What is Open Lear

Open Learning Guide 4

What is Open Learning?
An introduction to the series

Roger Lewis and Doug Spencer

 Council for Educational Technology

Published and distributed by the Council for Educational Technology,
3 Devonshire Street, London W1N 2BA.

First published 1986
ISBN 0 86184-126-3

© Council for Educational Technology 1986

Other than as permitted under the Copyright Act 1956, no part of this publication may be photocopied, recorded or otherwise reproduced, stored in a retrieval system or transmitted in any form by any electronic or mechanical means without the prior permission of the copyright owner.

Lewis, Roger, 1944–
 What is open learning? — (Open learning guide; 4)
 1. Distance education
 I. Title II. Spencer, Doug III. Series
 371.3   LC5800

ISBN 0-86184-126-3

Printed in Great Britain by H Charlesworth & Co Ltd
254 Deighton Road
Huddersfield HD2 1JJ

Contents

Preface	vii
Introduction	1
The Open Learning Guides	3
What this book covers	4
Acknowledgements	5
SECTION ONE. OPEN LEARNING	7
Introduction	9
A definition	9
Stages in the development of open learning	13
Some misconceptions dispelled	17
Conclusion	18
SECTION TWO. CENTRING ON THE LEARNER	21
Introduction	23
Learner-centred	23
Barriers as the learner sees them	24
Removing the barriers	26
Barriers: providers' assumptions	28
SECTION THREE. OPENNESS IN A SCHEME	35
Introduction	37
Learner choice	37
Using the table	38
SECTION FOUR. ADVANTAGES TO PROVIDERS AND EMPLOYERS	45
Introduction	47
Providers of specialist training and/or employers	48
Schools	50
Further and higher education	53
Adult and community education	54

SECTION FIVE. STAFF DEVELOPMENT AND THE OPEN
LEARNING GUIDES 57
Introduction 59
The challenge of open learning 59
New roles for staff in open learning 62
Staff development in open learning 65
Using the Guides 67

SECTION SIX. THE FUTURE OF OPEN LEARNING 71
Introduction 73
A multiplicity of providers and packages 74
An information technology base 76
Autonomous and experiential learning 76

SECTION SEVEN. JOB AIDS 81
Introduction 83
Learner flexibility profiles 83
Staff development profiles 87
An open learning toolkit 92

SECTION EIGHT. BOOKLIST AND GLOSSARY
TO THE OPEN LEARNING GUIDES 99
Booklist for the Open Learning Guides 101
Glossary for the Open Learning Guides 116

SECTION NINE. APPENDICES 127
Appendix One. Other initiatives and resources 129
Appendix Two. Definitions 130

Preface

Since 1975 the Council for Educational Technology has been continuously involved in the development of open-learning systems. The first stages of this work concentrated on 'non-advanced further education' and enabled the Council to make a major contribution to the National Extension College's 'FlexiStudy' system and other early developments, and incidentally to provide much advice and practical help in the form of publications and training workshops to lecturers who were finding their way into the new field of open learning. This experience (allied to that of the Open University) helped to provide the foundation upon which the 'Open Tech' programme (Manpower Services Commission) and PICKUP initiative (Department of Education and Science) are built, has led to the much more flexible approach now being taken by the Business and Technician Education Council and other validating bodies, and is recognized by the contract given to the Council by MSC to provide a training and support unit for Open Tech projects.

Maintaining the momentum of its work in open learning, the Council has moved into the fields of supported self-study in secondary schools and informal adult learning. In all this work over the past nine years, the Council has benefited from the cooperation and personal experience of an increasingly large group of experienced specialists in open learning and has, through its publications, attempted to make this experience available to lecturers, trainers and teachers who found themselves confronted with the need to get involved in open-learning methods.

This new series of Open Learning Guides is a further move in making the accumulated experience of those who have developed open-learning methods in the United Kingdom available to newcomers to the field. The series editor, Roger Lewis, has taken a lead in developments both through his work for the National Extension College and through his involvement from the beginning with the Council's own work. The drafts of the Guides have been commented on and improved by a process of consultation with several experts in the open-learning network, with the intention that the result will be a series of books which are directly helpful to those in industry, the professions, and adult, further and higher education who are called upon to develop and run open-learning schemes.

Norman Willis
Assistant Director
Council for Educational Technology
April 1984

Introduction

Introduction

THE OPEN-LEARNING GUIDES
This series of books is intended as a practical help to people setting up open-learning schemes, whether in education or training. The advice is deliberately aimed across the whole range of schemes and levels. The structure of the series is as follows.

WHAT IS OPEN LEARNING?

OPEN LEARNING IN ACTION: CASE STUDIES

MANAGEMENT	TUTORING	LEARNING MATERIAL
HOW TO DEVELOP AND MANAGE AN OPEN-LEARNING SCHEME	HOW TO TUTOR AND SUPPORT LEARNERS	HOW TO FIND AND ADAPT MATERIALS AND CHOOSE MEDIA
		HOW TO HELP LEARNERS ASSESS THEIR PROGRESS: HOW TO WRITE OBJECTIVES, SELF-ASSESSMENT QUESTIONS AND ACTIVITIES
		HOW TO COMMUNICATE WITH THE LEARNER
		HOW TO MANAGE THE PRODUCTION PROCESS

4 WHAT IS OPEN LEARNING?

The Guides thus cover the three main parts of most schemes: a management system, a tutorial support system and learning materials. Each book stands on its own but there are many areas of overlap and reference is made to other volumes in the series. In particular you are recommended to consult Volume 1, *Open Learning in Action*, as you use this text.

All the volumes except *Open Learning in Action* contain open-learning features. These include:

— objectives
— quiz sections which act as summaries
— activities to enable you to apply the principles to your work
— checklists to guide you whilst working through the activities
— job aids to use in running your scheme
— the provision of frequent examples and references to show how the ideas have been applied to particular cases.

These features are indicated in the text by introductory symbols to make them easily recognizable. Key words for this volume are defined in the Glossary (see Section Eight).

WHAT THIS BOOK COVERS

This volume starts with a definition of 'open learning' and illustrates this, drawing particularly on the *Open Learning in Action* book of case studies. The first section also gives a brief history of open learning and dispels some misconceptions. Section Two shows that 'openness' is a relative concept; schemes may be very open in one or two ways, fairly open in others and closed in yet others. The section identifies a number of barriers to particular groups of learners and shows how these can be removed and how learners can be helped to achieve greater autonomy. Section Three will help you to plan where your scheme should be open; or, if your scheme is running, to assess the ways in which it is currently open and to consider opening it further. Our analysis is based on aspects of openness, each of which can be scored.

While Sections Two and Three concentrate on advantages to the learner, Section Four focuses on the provider. Why should a school, a college, a training centre, a company or a professional organization offer open learning? Section Four considers the advantages open learning might offer to these providers.

Section Five begins with a discussion of the roles staff play in an open-learning scheme and goes on to list key skills and activities. It suggests how the Open Learning Guides might form a useful staff development aid. Section Six looks briefly into the future and Section Seven contains job aids and other resources to help you form a plan of action. Section Eight includes a booklist and comprehensive glossary of the terms used in the Open Learning Guides series. Section Nine includes two appendices — one on other initiatives and resources which the Open Learning Guides complement, and one on alternative terms for 'open learning'.

O | **Objectives**
As a result of this book you should be able to:
— define open learning

— decide which dimensions of openness are most important in your scheme
— use a range of tools to help you to estimate the degree of openness of your scheme
— draw up a plan of action to make your scheme more open (if necessary)
— assess the need for staff development in your scheme
— decide which other Open Learning Guides can help you
— plan ways of using the Open Learning Guides and related resources to carry out your plan of action
— estimate likely future developments in open learning.

Detailed objectives are given at the front of all the major sections of the book.

ACKNOWLEDGEMENTS
A team of readers very helpfully commented on this book in draft. The readers were:

John Coffey	Nigel Paine
Rob Littlejohn	Phil Race
Gaye Manwaring	Frances Robertson
Clive Neville	Philip Waterhouse

Janet Bollen prepared the reference aid to the series (see Section Eight) and dealt with the management of all stages, liaising with the many people involved.

Muriel Brooks and Joan Welch of the Council for Educational Technology saw the manuscript through production.

Section One. Open Learning

Open Learning

CONTENTS
Introduction
A definition
Stages in the development of open learning
Some misconceptions dispelled
Conclusion

INTRODUCTION
This section is divided into three main parts. The first answers the question 'What is open learning?'. We offer a definition, though with an invitation to adapt it to suit your own circumstances. The next part gives a brief sketch of some major developments in the history of open learning, including the influences of the Open University, the Council for Educational Technology and the Open Tech Programme of the Manpower Services Commission. The third part considers some common misconceptions held about open learning. For example, through equating it with traditional correspondence courses people fail to see its potential for meeting the needs of varied groups of learners in all areas of the curriculum.

O | **Objectives**
After working through this section you should be able to

— accept that 'open learning' is an umbrella term open to a variety of interpretations
— produce a definition of 'open learning' which suits you
— appreciate the richness of open learning by noting its development over the past 20 years and the variety of existing schemes
— see the possibilities for opening up your existing education or training provision
— extend your thinking on what it is possible to learn in the open mode.

A DEFINITION
First, what is the definition of open learning we are using in this book and throughout the Open Learning Guides? The definition is as follows.
 'Open learning' is a term used to describe courses flexibly designed to meet individual requirements. It is often applied to provision which tries to remove barriers that prevent attendances at more traditional courses, but it also suggests a learner-centred philosophy. Open-learning courses may be offered in a learning

centre of some kind or most of the activity may be carried out away from such a centre (eg, at home). In nearly every case specially prepared or adapted materials are necessary.
This definition needs some comment.

Course
Reference to the Glossary in this and other volumes in the series will show that the word 'course' is used to mean any planned learning experience. It does not necessarily imply a lengthy or academic programme. A 'course' may be a couple of hours' updating undertaken by a general practitioner, or a higher degree pursued over many years. A course may be tightly structured (as in the Open University undergraduate programme) or loose (eg, a group of learners coming together to discuss matters of common interest). A course may be academic or practical in content. It may aim to raise awareness, train, update or help someone get a qualification — or all of these. It may be a new way of packaging what already exists, or it may be composed of entirely new content. It may be offered by an educational, industrial or other provider or devised by the learner himself.

Activity
Decide which of these comes closest to the 'course' you are offering.

Checklist
In your definition have you considered:
— length
— structure
— purpose
— type of provider
— type of learner?

Individual requirements
Open learning is centred on the individual. Learning is a process undergone by individuals. But this does not mean that the learner is denied group interaction. Indeed, the experience of being part of a group may be an essential part of learning. Group experiences are essential parts of some open-learning schemes.

Removal of barriers
In the mid-1970s those wishing to forward the cause of open learning tended to concentrate on adults and on barriers preventing them from gaining access to conventional courses. Certain groups such as mothers at home, shiftworkers, and the disabled, could not easily attend education and training courses run in the traditional face-to-face mode. Open learning came to mean finding ways of removing these barriers, notably those of time and place.

Case-studies
In Volume 1, *Open Learning in Action,* the Telford, Peterborough and Luton schemes show how barriers have been removed in particular cases.

✶ Learner-centred philosophy
'Open learning' is now defined more positively. It not only lessens constraints and removes barriers; it also actively promotes such qualities in the learner as autonomy, independence and flexibility. Open learning thus now incorporates a strong learner-centred philosophy.

Activity
Decide whether your scheme is aimed primarily at removing barriers or developing learner autonomy, or whether the distinction is not helpful in your case.

Different bases for the learning
Some schemes are 'open' in that they provide flexible learning opportunities in a college, training centre or other institutional base. Individuals come to the centre to learn, usually from a range of specially selected resources. They are often helped by a counsellor or tutor. In other schemes the individual carries out some or most of his study at a distance from the institution.

Activity
Decide where learning will mainly take place in your scheme.

Checklist
Is it:

— home
— work
— a centre other than work
— mobile?

Specially prepared or adapted materials
The freedoms of open learning, such as those of time, pace and place, are usually made possible by giving the learner a package specially designed to enable him to learn on his own, for at least some of the time. There are exceptions to this, for example adult literacy provision is often one-to-one and self-help groups may not use learning materials. But these variants are less common, less visible. Usually at least part of the content and support is 'packaged'.

12 WHAT IS OPEN LEARNING?

Activity
Look back to the definition of open learning given in this section. If necessary, adapt or extend it to better convey your idea of what open learning means to you and/or your institution.

Here are some other definitions which have been given of the phrase 'open learning'.
From a paper by John Coffey, 'Open learning opportunities for mature students' in Working Paper 14, *Open Learning Systems for Mature Students*, by T Charles Davies, Council for Educational Technology, 1977: 'An Open Learning System is one in which the restrictions placed on students are under constant review and removed wherever possible. It incorporates the widest range of teaching strategies, in particular those using independent and individualized learning'.
From a workshop run by the National Extension College: 'Learning which is delivered at a time and place and through media which suit the needs and circumstances of the learner rather than of the institution'.
From the glossary of terms given on p 7 of *A New Training Initiative*, Manpower Services Commission, July 1984: 'Open learning: arrangements to enable people to learn at the time, place and pace which satisfies their circumstances and requirements. The emphasis is on opening up opportunities by overcoming barriers that result from geographical isolation, personal or work commitments or conventional course structures which have often prevented people from gaining access to the training they need'.
A range of recent open-learning activities reported in the press is shown below.

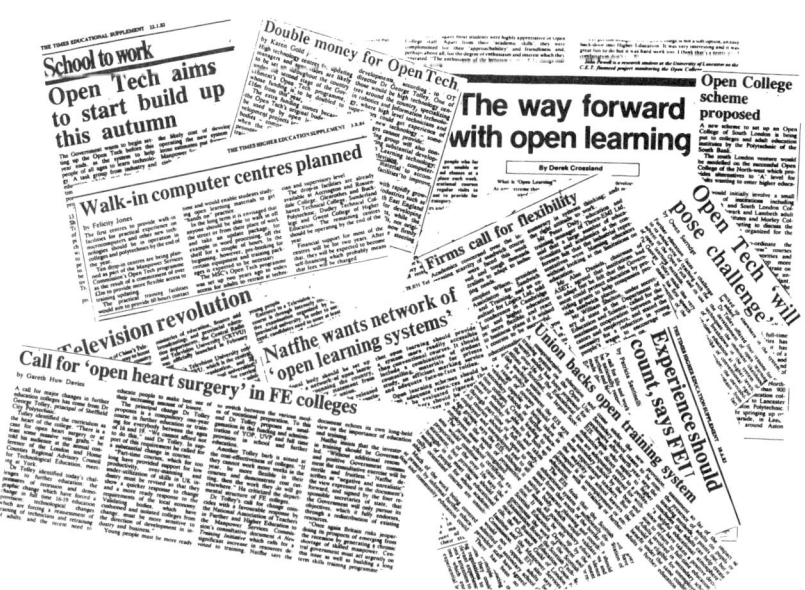

STAGES IN THE DEVELOPMENT OF OPEN LEARNING
We should remember that open features can be built into what may seem to be conventional courses. Traditional classes sometimes have qualities of openness. For example:

— learners can be given a choice of subject or topic
— learners can work for some of the time at their own pace
— textbooks and other materials can be carefully selected and adapted to suit the learners
— individuals can choose from a range of learning methods and ways of being assessed.

In adult education there is the potential, for example in Workers Educational Association classes, for learners to negotiate with the tutor the curriculum to be followed during class meetings. In our enthusiasm for openness we must not forget the opportunities for choice that exist in conventional systems. Some readers of this book will want to start by simply looking carefully at what they do now and encouraging learners to take advantage of existing opportunities.

This section looks at four main stages in the development of open learning. It presents a short and simplified sketch of how open learning has progressed over the past 20 years.

Correspondence courses
Many thousands of students — probably in excess of 100,000 — learn annually through one or other of the correspondence colleges. For many, correspondence study has been the only route to qualifications in professions such as accountancy and banking. Adults have been able to take GCE O- and A-levels and degrees by enrolling with correspondence colleges — assisted by the 'openness' of examining bodies in admitting 'external students' to their examinations, regardless of the learners' study route.

The Open University
But, apart from the notable exception of the National Extension College (set up as an educational trust in the early 1960s), the educational reputation of correspondence study has generally not been high. This was one of the main barriers the newly formed Open University had to overcome in the early 1970s. The difficulties of the University are well described in Walter Perry's *Open University*. Academics in other institutions attacked the very idea of an open university and mocked some of its principles, such as the importance of counselling and the learning potential offered by electronic media. But the new University acquired respectability in a remarkably short time: within five years many of its critics were surreptitiously using the course units as the basis for their own teaching; within another five the units were on reading lists, library shelves and in the hands of students of 'conventional' courses all over the country.

The OU has led by example. It developed the 'course team' as a means of producing high quality learning material. It created a regional structure to allow its students access to local tutors and counsellors. It brought the concept of counselling into correspondence study. Its students have been even more influential than its own academics in spreading open learning. The OU has brought respectability to open learning.

The Council for Educational Technology and other models of open learning

The very success of the OU gave rise to a major problem. The Open University brought to light more needs than it could possibly satisfy, and education and training institutions wanted to offer their own versions of open learning. They were starting from a very different position, with existing staff and structures. How could the education and training system offer open learning to new groups of students?

The Council for Educational Technology identified these issues in the mid-1970s and open learning began a new phase of development. Charles Davies in CET Working Paper 14 surveyed the models of openness that existed in the early 1970s — often small developments, barely noticed outside their own locality or industry:

— courses like that run by Doncaster College of Technology (as it then was) for quarry workers (see the case study in Volume 1, *Open Learning in Action*)
— distant learning schemes, like the SCOTBEC scheme for those living in the Highlands and Islands of Scotland
— private sector training schools in typing (see the Sight and Sound case study in Volume 1, *Open Learning in Action*)
— learning workshops similar to that described in the account of the Bradford Maths Workshop in Volume 1, *Open Learning in Action*
— 'learning by appointment' centres, often in colleges of further education.

Such schemes differed from the Open University in several ways. Generally they

— were small-scale
— had been developed to meet very specific needs
— included more sharply focused learning objectives
— offered a choice of modules
— allowed learners to start at more or less any time.

CET, through its Open Learning Systems programme, fostered these developments. It grouped the schemes it supported into three, based on the location of learners relative to the institution. These are set out in the table opposite.

The classification was first developed by D C Spencer in CET Working Paper 19, *Thinking About Open-Learning Systems,* pp 31–2. Many current schemes are, though, mixtures of the features of more than one type. And new models are becoming apparent. For example, Dean and Whitlock (1985) suggest a range of possible venues when the presenting medium is the computer:

— on-the-job: the learner uses the equipment he will use later, when carrying out the job for which he is being trained
— by-the-job: the learner uses equipment set aside for the training function
— training centre: the learner studies at the same venue as is used for conventional training
— learning centre: the learner studies at a centre purpose-designed for open-learning use
— mobile work station: the equipment is transported in a car or van to wherever the learner is based.

Type of scheme	Typical features	Examples in 'Open Learning in Action'
Institution-based/ 'workshop'	Provision of an organized collection of learning materials and the means to use them; tutorial/counselling guidance available; range of ability catered for; learners 'drop in', book or are timetabled; learners work at own pace; long opening hours; emphasis on learning by doing. Learners are already members of the institution or live near enough to it to drop in frequently if necessary. Group work is possible as well, eg, in adjoining rooms.	Bradford Maths Workshop; Sight and Sound
Local	Learners live near enough to an institution to attend on at least an occasional basis. For most of the time learners use open-learning materials, eg, those produced by the National Extension College. The institution offers counselling, tuition and access to resources.	Telford; Luton; Peterborough
Distant	Learners live in widely dispersed locations, not local to the providing institution. Learning is heavily dependent on a package, a distant tutor and telephone/post contact with centre. Residential periods of study are also often offered.	Doncaster; Cement and Concrete; Dundee

Case-study

In Volume 1, *Open Learning in Action*, the zookeepers' course uses distant tutors to mark the work of learners all over the UK. But each learner also has a 'zoo tutor' to support practical work and to carry out related assessment.

The Open University's Health and Parent Education courses are centrally produced but are then used in many different ways. Much of their success in attracting new audiences can be attributed to the local delivery of the learning in informal groups.

Classification of open learning according to the physical location of learner relative to centre no longer adequately describes the richness of open learning. Sometimes there may be no obvious providing centre. Learning exchanges, for example, enable two or more individuals to swap skills. Self-help groups of learners meet informally to discuss issues and solve problems with little or no help from professionals. Perhaps the most open of all open learning is the individual himself working on his own programme using either specially designed resources (eg, a structured learning text, a computer program) or just any resources he has to hand. The research of Alan Tough has shown the remarkable extent of such self-learning undertaken by all adults. They complete their own learning projects and acquire either a specific skill, such as brewing beer, or a more diverse and complex set of capacities, such as those involved in child-rearing. They may, at any stage, encounter a providing institution, such as a college or training centre.

The work of the Council for Educational Technology was remarkably successful. Much is owed to the energy and enthusiasm of key individuals who, in the mid-1970s, spent much time speaking at meetings and enthusing people in all sectors, but particularly in further education colleges. The most successful innovation in terms of numbers was FlexiStudy, a local open-learning scheme, developed by the Council for Educational Technology, the National Extension College and Barnet College. This can now claim to be a national network, with nearly 200 colleges and other institutions providing learners with support as they study mainly from NEC materials. (See FlexiStudy Pack under the National Extension College in the Booklist.)

The Open Tech Programme
The collaborative nature of schemes such as FlexiStudy attracted the Manpower Services Commission when it considered its own entry into open learning in the early 1980s. Significantly, it chose a very decentralized model, with funding dispersed to products of widely different kinds based in institutions of many different types. 'Collaboration', 'cooperation', 'sharing' were the key words. The Open Tech Programme is still in an early stage (1985) but it has introduced some new emphases to open learning. (See Open Tech Unit in the Booklist.) These include

— funding 'delivery' projects, to take existing learning material and use this as the base for meeting the needs of local industrial and commercial training
— establishing 'practical training facilities' to overcome the problem of providing hands-on experience
— encouraging some centres to produce open-learning materials to a very high standard of presentation
— encouraging providers to make materials available in very small chunks
— a relative unconcern with formal accreditation, and consequent pressure on the validating bodies such as the Business and Technician Education Council to relax their regulations
— a focus on high technology delivery and communications media
— an emphasis on marketing and self-sustainability (Open Tech projects are expected to earn income in order to survive after a limited period of grant aid)
— establishing support projects such as the Materials and Resources Information Service (MARIS) to serve open learning generally and to spread openness throughout the UK's system of education and training.

SOME MISCONCEPTIONS DISPELLED

This section dispels some misconceptions about open learning. These are summarized below. We comment briefly and refer you to relevant case studies in Volume 1, *Open Learning in Action*.

Misconception	Comment

Open learning and distance learning are one and the same	Open learning sometimes uses some features of distance learning, eg, specially prepared materials and a support system for learners. But the two terms are not synonymous. Distance learning is a sub-category of open learning. Distance learning usually implies geographical distance between learner and providing institution. The learner makes contact by post or telephone with the institution and with any tutor.
	    Open-learning schemes can be set up in institutions which students/employees attend full-time, as in the workshops described earlier in this section. So geographical distance is not essential for a scheme to be described as 'open learning'.
	    Check the variety of schemes described in Volume 1, *Open Learning in Action*. Note particularly the Bradford and Sight and Sound examples.

Open learning is part-time	Open learning can be used for full-time as well as part-time students. See the example of Bradford in Volume 1, *Open Learning in Action*.
Open learning is confined to formally enrolled students	Learners need not necessarily enrol with an institution. See the 'Small Businesses' example in Volume 1, *Open Learning in Action*.
Open learning is suitable only for adults	Open learning arrangements can work in schools. In Volume 1, *Open Learning in Action*, see the example of Clwyd. See, too, the books by Waterhouse in the Booklist.
In open-learning schemes the learner is isolated	Open learners can work in groups as well as on their own. Sometimes residential study is provided. In Volume 1, *Open Learning in Action*, see the 'self-help' groups described in the OU Health Education case study; and also Dundee and Doncaster case studies (for residential study).

Feedback is always delayed in open learning	Some open schemes provide instant feedback — eg, from a tutor in a learning workshop. The use of telecommunications and computers can mean very fast feedback even across a geographical distance (eg, via MAIL). In Volume 1, *Open Learning in Action*, see the case studies of the Bradford Maths Workshop and the BBC.
Open learning is a poor substitute for face-to-face teaching and thus produces less successful results	Results can be much better by open learning. See the figures given in case studies in Volume 1, *Open Learning in Action*, eg, Cement and Concrete Association, Telford, British Telecom, Clwyd.
Open learning is unsuitable for practical subjects	Open learning is here confused with distance learning. Also, the statement forgets that it is possible to build in face-to-face sessions and on-job support to guide practical learning. The package, too, can be skilfully designed to help learners master practical skills, eg, via a home experiment kit. In Volume 1, *Open Learning in Action*, see the case studies on Zoo Animal Management and Sight and Sound. Also see Chapter 13, 'Hands-on requirements' in John Twining's *Open Learning for Technicians*.
Open learning is unsuitable for skills which involve interaction between people	The same comment applies as in the previous box. In Volume 1, *Open Learning in Action*, see the YMCA case study.
Open learning is just correspondence education with a new name	Look at the range of open-learning schemes described in Volume 1, *Open Learning in Action*.

CONCLUSION

The following is a summary list of the characteristic features of an open-learning scheme:

— a focus on the learner's own purposes and on helping the learner to articulate these at every stage (they are often practical and problem- or task-centred)
— a commitment to helping the learner to acquire independence and autonomy
— a focus on the learner's own environment and experience — domestic, social, communal and work-based — and on its potential for learning
— the belief that the learner is self-directed, that individual learning styles need to be

respected and used, that learning involves the whole person (see Rogers, 1983, in the Booklist)
— the use of professionals to facilitate learning (rather than to teach), and to mobilize the learners themselves, eg, into self-help groups
— the use of objectives to underpin course planning; these are known to, and ideally changeable by, the learner
— the use of very frequent assessment, primarily to help the learner to achieve his objectives and to monitor his progress
— the absence of unnecessary entry requirements
— the use of new technology to bridge the distance between learner and provider.

For elaboration, see Wedermeyer's book in the Booklist. For self-help groups see the packs produced by the National Extension College (details in the Booklist, under Lewis and Paine).

Quiz

1. Pick out *three* features of open learning that are important to you.

2. Which of the following comes closest to the definition of 'course' used in this book

(a) an academic programme
(b) a planned learning experience
(c) a tightly structured training event?

3. Two of the following statements are correct, according to this section. Which are they?

(a) In setting up the Open Tech Programme the MSC followed the Open University model.
(b) Open learning can operate without the involvement of educators and trainers.
(c) Sitting an O-level as an external student is an example of open learning.
(d) Open learning always involves study at home.

4. 'Open learning is unsuitable for young students and for practical subjects.' Do you agree? Give a reason for your view.

Answers
1. Those stressed in the text include: the removal of barriers, a learner-centred philosophy, a variety of places at which the learning can be undertaken, the use of specially prepared materials. See too the Conclusion to this section.

2. (b) is the definition given in this book. (a) is too limited; the programme need not be academic. An open-learning course can be loosely structured and need not be training — so (c) is mistaken on two counts.

3. (b) and (c) are correct. Here are some comments on the four statements.

(a) We argue that the MSC established the Open Tech on a different model, that of collaboration between existing institutions. The Open Tech Unit is not a central institution like the Open University.
(b) Yes — as in study groups, self-help groups, learning exchanges.
(c) We would argue 'yes'. The O-level is 'open' to learners regardless of their method of study. They may, for example, study entirely on their own without the help of any teacher. This is an open dimension. Other aspects may be closed, for example, in O-level the syllabus has to be taken by the learner as a given.
(d) No. Some schemes, such as the Bradford Maths Workshop, make learning materials flexibly available in a learning centre. Open-learning courses may be studied in a wide variety of places, as well as, or instead of, at home.

4. We would not agree. We would point to successful examples of open-learning schemes for younger students, eg, the Clwyd case study in Volume 1, *Open Learning in Action,* and in practical areas of the curriculum, eg, the Zoo Animal Management study in the same book. Open learning is flexible enough to cater for most needs, depending on the imagination and resourcefulness of the course designer.

Section Two. Centring on the Learner

Centring on the Learner

CONTENTS
Introduction
Learner-centred
Barriers as the learner sees them
Removing the barriers
Barriers: providers' assumptions

INTRODUCTION
This section looks more closely at open learning. We begin by stressing what lies at the heart of open learning: it is centred on the individual learner. Much existing provision of education and training is, in one way or another, awkward or inappropriate for the learner. We identify four such barriers to learning: physical, educational, individual and financial. These are themselves partly created by assumptions held by the bodies that provide education and training. We go on to look at ways of removing these barriers, or lessening their effect. We make the point that open learning is a relative concept: schemes are not totally open or totally closed. This is explored more thoroughly in Section Three.

Objectives
After working through this section you should be able to:

— identify barriers to learning that may exist in current provision
— identify ways in which providers create or contribute to these barriers
— suggest ways in which the barriers may be removed
— explain why and how 'open' is a relative concept
— apply the content of this section to your own scheme.

LEARNER-CENTRED
Open learning puts the learner at the centre and works out from there. Volume 5 of this series, *How to Develop and Manage an Open-Learning Scheme* shows how this principle should be borne in mind at every phase of the design and operation of a scheme.

All arrangements — learning materials, administrative contacts, support system — should work in the best interests of the learner, helping him to acquire greater autonomy.

Much conventional provision would claim similar ends to those of open learning — more learner independence, greater learner flexibility and decision-making capacity and so on. But there are barriers in the way in which conventional provision

Extract from 'The Open Learning Toolkit: a development aid for managers', published by the National Extension College on behalf of the Manpower Services Commission, 1985, and reproduced by permission of the College (Crown copyright 1985)

is arranged, not only barriers to learner access but also barriers to the acquisition of greater autonomy once the learner enrols. Open learning tries to remove such barriers.

But first, how do the barriers appear to the intending learner?

BARRIERS AS THE LEARNER SEES THEM

The barriers can be summarized under four headings: physical, educational, individual and financial. These overlap, but it is convenient to consider them separately.

Physical/time barriers

The course may not be available within reasonable travelling distance. Necessary resources, such as up-to-date machinery, may not be available locally. Or the course may be offered locally but the learner may still not be able to attend it because of personal circumstances such as family responsibilities, work patterns or his employer's policy on release. The day and time of meetings (eg, each Tuesday for two hours at 9.00) may not be convenient. The beginning and end of the course may be fixed and thus access to the education/training may not be possible at many times of the year.

Education/training design

The education/training design of the provision may not necessarily match the learner's needs. There may be no scope for the learner who wants only to brush up his knowledge. The course may be designed in such a way that the learner has to pay for, and attend, 20 sessions in order to get access to the chunk he actually wants. Once in the scheme, the learner may have to accept one pace through the material, covering everything in equal depth.

The individual

The individual himself may be unable to take advantage of what is offered. This may be for a variety of reasons such as lack of awareness, reluctance to attend a class in case he is 'shown up' in front of others, lack of confidence. It may have been a long time since he studied anything. His memories of being a 'student' may be negative, dating from times when he was 'taught' against his will. He may lack the entry requirements set by the institution; especially educational qualifications which, if he is an adult, he may not have had the chance to acquire. Some of these problems may be cleared up by advice and counselling, but this may not be available in the right place and at the right time.

Financial

Financial barriers are fairly easy to define. A course may cost too much for the learner. He may not be eligible for a grant or for employer support. Travel and other costs may be prohibitive.

Costs can also be too great for people other than the learner: for example, the employer may not be able or prepared to release the learner from work because it would be too expensive in terms of staff replacements or lost production.

The four sets of barriers are summarized in the table below.

Barrier	Example
Physical/time	Location of course Times of classes Times of exam
Educational	Content of course Sequencing of content Method of delivery Inappropriate objectives
Individual	Lack of awareness of what is available Lack of confidence Entry requirements
Financial	Cost of travel and fees Cost of release from employment

26 WHAT IS OPEN LEARNING?

Activity

Consider your target learners. Which of the above barriers are *you* concerned to remove?

REMOVING THE BARRIERS

In the real world it is impossible to remove every constraint or barrier mentioned earlier. What matters is to remove as many as possible of those barriers which make access to learning difficult. In the case-studies printed in Volume 1, *Open Learning in Action*, you will note that schemes tackle barriers that significantly and adversely affect their target groups. Some examples are given below.

Scheme	Barrier	Action
Clwyd LEA A-level Sociology	New subjects at A-level in demand but cannot be offered in school because of lack of specialist teachers.	Prepare subject-matter package; use central distant tutors on a part-time basis; develop and use existing support services within each school
Luton/Telford/ Peterborough FlexiStudy	Adults cannot attend conventional classes.	Use 'bought in' or home-produced materials, studied at home; tutoring available by post, telephone and occasional visit to college.
Telford	Students over 18 are not given day-release. Course requires three evening classes a week.	Combine FlexiStudy provision with one evening class each week.
Dundee College of Education	Learners cannot be released to take the courses in conventional form.	Prepare high-quality package; add support from a tutor and links to learner's own job.
Leicester Pharmacy Project	Attendance at conventional provision is inconvenient/ impossible.	Modular package — learner not committed to a long course or to attendance.

Schemes may be open in some ways but not in others. Some examples are given below, again from Volume 1, *Open Learning in Action*.

Scheme	Open characteristics	Closed characteristics
OU undergraduate programme	No entry requirements. Study at home.	Must be over 21 years of age; fixed assignment and exam dates; must start February; may have to attend a summer school.
British Telecom	Can study at home and at convenience of the individual.	Must work for British Telecom and be approved by the employer; fixed dates for phase tests.
BBC Computer Literacy	Anyone can use the resources (television programmes, books, etc).	Access to computer necessary to achieve many objectives.
Bradford Maths Workshop	Long hours of access.	Learners not allowed to remove materials from the workshop.

Here is one of the case-studies analysed in more detail from this point of view — the Dundee College of Education Diploma of Educational Technology.

Open characteristics	Closed characteristics
Place of study Pace of study Completion date Some choice of sequence and topics of study units Projects and assignments can be negotiated with tutors College blocks allow for individual timetable and choice of activities	Start date Must be in employment (for project work) Must pass entry test All assignments, and a project, must be completed Dates of college blocks

Sometimes what looks like a closed characteristic is deliberately designed into a scheme for the benefit of learners. An example is pacing, used in some schemes to help learners to keep up. At other times, a closed characteristic is the result of lack of resources — eg, the Cement and Concrete Association allows telephone contact on only one evening for this reason. We shall look further at open/closed characteristics in Section Three.

28 WHAT IS OPEN LEARNING?

Activity
Where does *your* scheme need to be open? Where should it be closed? For what reasons?

BARRIERS: PROVIDERS' ASSUMPTIONS

Colleges and training centres make certain assumptions which tend to limit the openness of provision. Some of these are set out below, together with suggestions for more positive policies. The list is based on tables in *Flexible Learning Opportunities*, Further Education Unit, 1983 — see the Booklist.

Assumptions	More positive policies	Some practical steps	Case study in 'Open Learning in Action'
Philosophical The learner should be dependent on a providing institution; learner learns in a group; learner can't be trusted to work on his own; part of the necessary discipline is to fit in with the customs of the provider.	Make clear commitment to learner.	Review the extent of learner autonomy on current course provision.	YMCA; Peterborough. (See also the studies of Portsmouth and East Devon in Birch and Latcham, 1984a, in the Booklist.)
Limited view of teacher-trainer activity Teacher transmits a message to learners collected in a group, the teacher is 'working' when addressing a class — other work is preparatory to, and consequent on, this.	Define role of teacher/trainer more flexibly.	Contact by telephone and new technologies as well as in formal classes; allocate time for preparing course material for independent study.	Luton; Telford; Peterborough; Bradford Maths Workshop.
Limited view of learner activity Learners attend and receive the teacher's message; they absorb as much of it as they can and 'take notes'.	More flexible attitude to the process of learning.	Negotiation of objectives; use of wider range of resources and of new delivery methods; choice of sequence; use of projects.	Dundee; Telford.
	More flexible assessment methods.	Self- and peer- as well as teacher-assessment.	YMCA

Single controlling agency The college/training centre works on its own.	Collaborative models with local industry.	Courses planned and run jointly in firms and in colleges.	Doncaster; Small business; Zoo Animal Management.
Restricted target population Learners are defined in terms of prior education and/or intended qualification/ vocation.	Attract new groups; recognize life experience as well as qualifications.	Develop marketing programme; make entry requirements more flexible.	Luton; Telford.
Set management pattern Legal, administrative and financial regulations and customs make it difficult to implement more open methods.	Make the management and administration more flexible.	Make facilities available for more hours per day, days per week, weeks per year.	Peterborough; Bradford Maths Workshop; Sight and Sound.

The following quotations show some of these more positive policies in action.

A new role for the tutor

> The role of a tutor in the Workshop is quite different from that of a teacher in a traditional classroom. First of all, what the tutor does in a conventional classroom is private, a matter of concern only to himself and his students. In the Workshop tutors have to work alongside one another. Secondly, the classroom teacher decides in advance exactly what he is going to teach; he prepares the lesson and usually sticks closely to his plan. He controls the learning from beginning to end. In the Workshop it is the student who controls the learning and he initiates contact with the teacher who must thus be ready for anything.

Extract from 'The Bradford Mathematics Workshop' in 'Open Learning in Action', Open Learning Guide 1, p 117, edited by Roger Lewis and published by the Council for Educational Technology, 1984

A flexible attitude to the process of learning

> We are now therefore concentrating on one-off books to ensure greater flexibility of use and are also focusing on relevance. In these ways we are giving more weight to the point of view of our users — busy people who are impatient of theory and who need an immediate pay-off.

Extract from 'Leicester Pharmacy Project' in 'Open Learning in Action', Open Learning Guide 1, p 113, edited by Roger Lewis and published by the Council for Educational Technology, 1984

> Throughout the course, students are asked to talk about some part of their work as keepers and to carry out relevant activities. The activities are important because students learn best — and enjoy learning most — when they are *doing* something.
>
> The task book will guide students and senior staff engaged in training. The student will be expected to complete about 25 tasks of those presented in the book. The senior staff in the zoo will use the book to check that an appropriate balance of practical work has been competently carried out.

Extract from 'Zoo Animal Management Open-Learning Scheme' in 'Open Learning in Action', Open Learning Guide 1, pp 78 and 82, edited by Roger Lewis and published by the Council for Educational Technology, 1984

> We knew that although the aim of the television series would be explanation, the amount of learning that would take place as a result of the programmes themselves would be limited. It was planned to broadcast the series both to adults at home and to classes in schools and colleges. But although the institutional audience could be expected to use the series fairly systematically it was unlikely that this would be the case for home viewers.
>
> Each broadcast would therefore have to be effective as an independent presentation. This posed big production problems, since a good deal of technical explanation would be needed, and the capacity of a single 25-minute television programme to convey complicated ideas is not very great. It is normal for our educational programmes to be accompanied by a range of supporting materials and links with other means of learning and this was clearly going to be very important to the success of this project. We would need to plan for books, for linked classes and courses, for an information service and possibly for computer hardware and software as well.

Extract from 'BBC Computer Literacy Project 1979–83' in 'Open Learning in Action', Open Learning Guide 1, p 5, edited by Roger Lewis and published by the Council for Educational Technology, 1984

Attracting new clients

> My client audience was now growing clearer. It included shift workers, mums-at-home and people whose jobs involved a lot of travel, such as air hostesses and sales staff. Many of these were mature students who didn't want to expose their — supposed — ignorance in front of younger learners, preferring the anonymity of distance learning. Local employers also indicated that flexible learning opportunities for their employees would be welcome, to cater for production and working conditions.

Extract from 'Open Learning at Luton College of Higher Education' in 'Open Learning in Action', Open Learning Guide 1, p 190, edited by Roger Lewis and published by the Council for Educational Technology, 1984

Catering for small numbers

> The rest of our open learning is largely designed to meet the problems of small numbers. Over two years ago I decided that from the beginning of the next session any course or option which had normally recruited five or fewer was to be converted to FlexiStudy.

Extract from 'Open Learning at Peterborough Technical College' in 'Open Learning in Action', Open Learning Guide 1, p 237, edited by Roger Lewis and published by the Council for Educational Technology, 1984

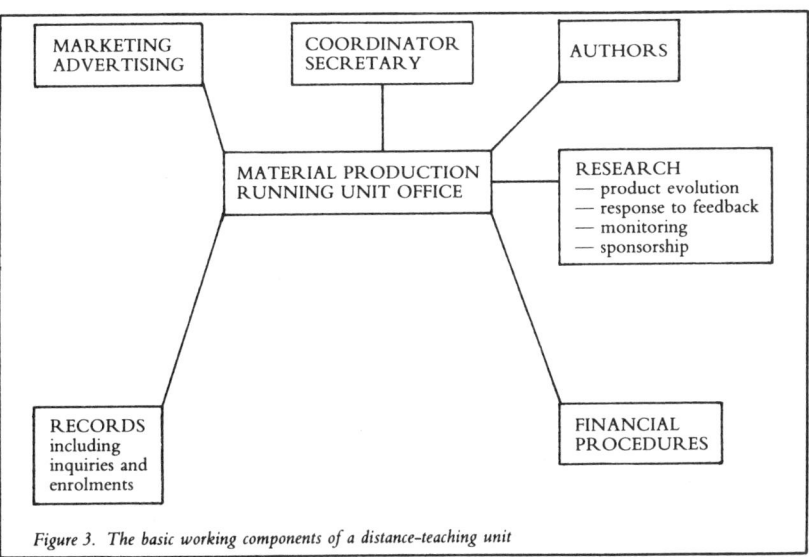

Figure 3. *The basic working components of a distance-teaching unit*

Extract from 'Leicester Pharmacy Project' in 'Open Learning in Action', Open Learning Guide 1, p 108, edited by Roger Lewis and published by the Council for Educational Technology, 1984

Self-help groups

> Just as important as the support provided by the health professionals and local coordinators is the support provided by other learners. The self-help group system was set up to enable students to share their experiences and to help each other — although those who wish to study alone or with a friend or neighbour are perfectly free to do so.
>
> The typical self-help group is formed specially for the course, has about five or six members and meets in someone's house about once a fortnight.
>
> Self-help groups, in fact, provide participants with a secure, non-threatening environment in which their own attitudes and behaviour can be challenged and be either modified or reinforced.

Extract from 'The Open University Health Education Programme' in 'Open Learning in Action', Open Learning Guide 1, pp 134 and 135, edited by Roger Lewis and published by the Council for Educational Technology, 1984

32 WHAT IS OPEN LEARNING?

> I feel it is necessary to introduce a new student to others who are following the same course. This in turn develops self-help groups which are an integral part of this approach to learning. There are two tutorial rooms on the periphery of the Workshop which are often used by the students to meet in this way.

Extract from 'The Bradford Mathematics Workshop' in 'Open Learning in Action', Open Learning Guide 1, p 146, edited by Roger Lewis and published by the Council for Educational Technology, 1984

Quiz

1. Below are two lists. The left-hand list is of types of barrier; the right-hand list gives examples of these types. Match up the lists so the examples are paired with the appropriate type of barrier.

(a) Educational
(b) Financial
(c) Individual
(d) Physical/time

(i) the classes are in an inaccessible location
(ii) a learner lacks study skills
(iii) the presentation is too academic
(iv) the employer cannot afford to release his workforce

2. Which of the following statements is correct, according to the text?

(a) Open-learning schemes by definition are able to remove all barriers to learning.

(b) Open-learning schemes are usually open in some ways and closed in others.

3. On the left, below, is a list of providers' assumptions. On the right, a list of ways in which these assumptions may be opened up. Find *one* relevant example from the second list for each item on the left.

(a) limited view of teacher/ trainer activity
(b) limited view of learner activity
(c) single controlling agency

(d) restricted target population

(i) learners are asked to state their objectives, at start of course
(ii) course content is re-jigged to suit additional occupations
(iii) the college provides tuition; the local employer provides access to modern equipment
(iv) learners are sent questionnaires on the degree of convenience of the provision, with a view to redesigning the course

(e) set management pattern

(f) philosophical

(v) learners carry out a work-based project, with line managers supervising some aspects of progress
(vi) the teacher/trainer is given time to prepare learning materials
(vii) the teacher facilitates and provides feedback
(viii) the course is offered regularly, regardless of numbers enrolling at any one time.

Answers
1. (a) and (iii)
(b) and (iv)
(c) and (ii)
(d) and (i)
These are the pairs we intended though you may have other matches. As we say in the text, there is considerable overlap between categories.

2. (a) may be an ideal to strive for. (b) is the statement that most accurately reflects the situation in practice.

3. There are many possible combinations. We would choose: (a) and (vi), (b) and (i), (c) and (iii), (d) and (ii), (e) and (viii), (f) and (iv). Here are comments on our choices.

(a) and (vi). (vi) shows a recognition that the teacher/trainer's role is more diverse than giving lectures to classes.

(b) and (i). (i) shows that the learner is being expected to take a more active role than merely to sit and listen.

(c) and (iii). This seems like a genuinely collaborative approach, with each agency (college and employer) contributing from a position of strength.

(d) and (ii). This shows an attempt to attract additional clients to the course.

(e) and (viii). Waiting for a 'viable group' is an indication of a set management pattern. (viii) shows a commitment to overcome this custom. It is the approach described in the case study of Peterborough Technical College, in Volume 1, *Open Learning in Action*.

(f) and (iv). This might seem more obscure than the others. (iv) shows the provider seeking the views of the clients. If the questionnaire response merits it, the course will be redesigned to fit more exactly the needs and preferences of the target group. It is thus learner-centred in philosophy.

There are other possibilities.

(v) could be matched with (a) — presumably the teacher/trainer is involved but in a new way, sharing responsibility with the line manager.

Or with (b) — the learner is engaged in an active way, by a work-based project.

Or with (c) — a work-based supporter is used.

Or with (f) — if the commitment to using work as a learning focus breaks new philosophical ground.

Depending on the context, (vii) could belong with (a) or (f), or even with (e).

There are many other possibilities. You may like to check your own pairs in the light of the above discussion.

Section Three. Openness in a Scheme

Openness in a Scheme

CONTENTS
Introduction
Learner choice
Using the table

INTRODUCTION
This section will help you to plan where your scheme should be open. Or, if your scheme is running, to assess the ways in which it is currently open and to consider opening it further. Our analysis is based on aspects of openness, each of which can be scored. The approach is elaborated in Section Seven (see p 83).

Objectives
After working through this section you should be able to

— identify open and closed aspects in a scheme
— identify the extent to which a scheme is open on a particular aspect.

LEARNER CHOICE
The learner has a career, beginning before entry to a scheme and ending (in a sense) when he leaves the scheme (see Volume 3, *How to Tutor and Support Learners*). This is shown in the diagram below, together with typical questions the learner asks at each of these stages.

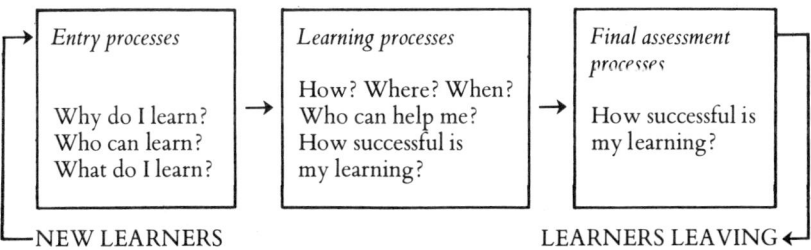

Early attempts to define 'open learning' emphasized ease of access and availability. This implied that freedom was provided to the learner mainly in terms of the 'when?' and 'where?' of study. Nowadays a much broader definition is given to openness. Increased autonomy means that the learner exercises choice on many aspects of learning, at every stage of his course. He may choose:

38 WHAT IS OPEN LEARNING?

WHY he learns: his choice to learn is his own.
WHAT he learns: he chooses or formulates his own objectives and content.
HOW he learns: he chooses the methods and route to suit his own way of learning.
WHERE he learns: he chooses the learning environment which will work out best for *him*.
WHEN he learns: he chooses when to start, his pace, when to finish.
HOW his learning will be measured: he decides *when* to subject his learning to assessment, *what sort* of assessment — eg, self-assessment or formal, *who* will help him to carry out assessment).
WHO can help him: he decides who is best placed to help, and when.
WHAT he does next: he decides what he want to do next (further courses, jobs).

In a completely open system, the learner can learn whatever he wishes, for whatever reasons, wherever he chooses, however he chooses. But schemes are never totally open in all these ways.

The following table shows how each of our basic questions has several aspects. For each aspect we have set out a continuum: the left-hand side is closed and the right-hand side is open. We then give an example from Volume 1, *Open Learning in Action*, of a scheme that is relatively open on each aspect.

USING THE TABLE
You can use the table as an aid, for example:

— to plan a scheme that is open where you want it to be
— to revise a scheme that is closed where it needs to be open
— to analyse the openness of a particular scheme on each aspect.

The table shows only the two extreme points of each aspect, ie, the open and the closed. There are several possible points in between. These may be shown by marking a point along the line or by using numbered staging points, as in the following examples.

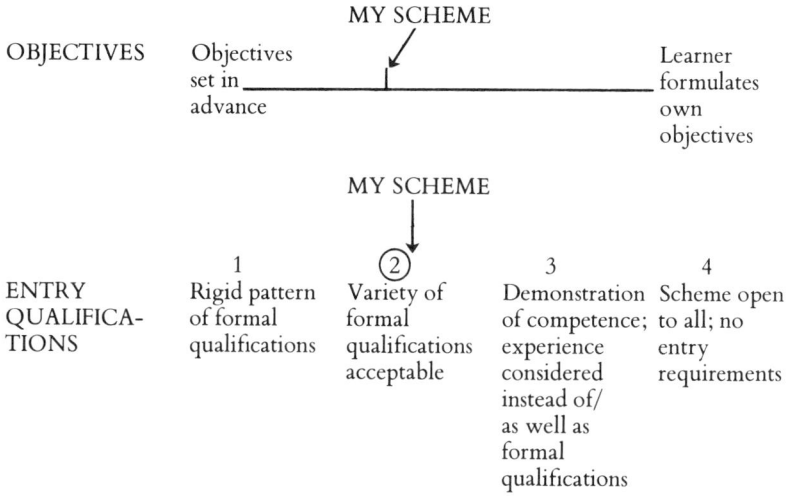

Basic question	Closed ———————————→ Aspects ———————————→ Open		Example from 'Open Learning in Action'
Who?	Scheme open to select groups only	Scheme open to all	BBC Computer Literacy Project
	Set entry requirements, eg, traditional exam success	Self-assessment and diagnostic facilities	Bradford Maths Workshop
	Scheme not marketed	Extensive publicity, information regularly updated	BBC Computer Literacy Project
Why?	Choice made by others, eg, tutor, employer	Learner choice	Open University Health Education
	No counselling or guidance	Pre-entry counselling	Dundee College of Education
What?	Entire syllabus set out in advance, eg, by validating body; no choice possible within it	Learner formulates own objectives	Small Businessmen
	Limited to materials the tutor/provider has produced	Uses wide range of materials drawn from many sources	BBC Computer Literacy Project
	Whole course must be taken	Content tailored to need; individual learners can take different modules	Bradford Maths Workshop

How?	No guidance on selection of content	Guidance on selection of content	Bradford Maths Workshop
	Knowledge, facts, 'academic'	Experience, practice, feeling, attitude	YMCA
	No recognition of past experience	Credit given for past experience	YMCA
	Only one method/style provided for; little variation in learner activity	Choice of learning methods/styles; varied activities	BBC Computer Literacy Project; YMCA
	One route only through material	Choice of routes through material	Bradford Maths Workshop
	Package in one medium only	Package uses variety of media	Open University Health Education
Where?	One place only (eg, at work)	Learner chooses place/anywhere (eg, home, work, while travelling)	Cement and Concrete Association
	Regular fixed attendance required	No attendance required	Leicester Pharmacy Project
	Practical work requires fixed attendance	Practical work offered through kits and/or drop-in access and/or place of work itself	Zoo Animal Management

When?	Fixed starting dates	Start any time	Sight and Sound
	Learner paced by a fixed timetable	Learner decides pace of work	Open University Health Education
	Fixed ending	End at any time	Leicester Pharmacy Project
How is the learner doing?	Externally fixed method of assessment, eg, formal exam	Variety of assessment methods; learner chooses assessment methods; learner constructs method of assessment	BBC Computer Literacy Project
	Normative assessment	Criteria/competency-based assessment	Bradford Maths Workshop
	No feedback on performance	Frequent, full, ongoing feedback on performance	Telford College of FE
	Assessment dates fixed and non-negotiable	Learner decides when to be assessed	Bradford Maths Workshop
	Assessment available only for whole course	Assessment available for each module	Bradford Maths Workshop
Who can help the learner?	No support outside package	Variety of possible kinds of support provided (eg, advice, guidance counselling)	Open University Health Education

	Only professional supporters (eg, teachers) encouraged	Non-professional, as well as professional supporters; informal as well as formal support encouraged (eg, mentor, family, friends)	BBC Computer Literacy Project
	Support available only in one place, eg, training centre	Support available wherever possible	Open University Health Education
	No choice of supporter	Learner can choose supporter	Open University Health Education
	Support available in one mode only, eg, face-to-face	Support available by a variety of modes, eg, learner, telephone, face-to-face	Doncaster Assisted Private Study
What does it lead to?	One destination	Various possible destinations	Computer Literacy Project BBC; Open University Health Education; FlexiStudy

Notes

1. It is possible to increase or to reduce the number of basic questions you use to analyse a scheme.
2. It is also possible to increase or to reduce the number of aspects of each question. You can see, for example, that we give two aspects for Why? and six for What?
3. All schemes will be open on some aspects, closed on others — either through choice or through lack of resources.
4. Some parts of a scheme, eg, different modules or practical work, may be open to a different extent, or in different ways, from other parts of the same scheme.

You can have any number of staging points. Look back to the first aspect of What? This is divided into five stages in the example below.

	1	2	3	4	5
OBJECTIVES	Objectives set in advance; no choice possible	Compulsory 'core' objectives; learner chooses any additional objectives	Learner selects from listed objectives, free choice	Learner negotiates objectives with a tutor	Learner formulates own objectives

Here are some further examples of aspects divided up in this way.

	1	2	3	4
ATTENDANCE	Regular attendance required on set dates	Regular attendance but dates negotiable	Attendance but minimal/infrequent/at learner's convenience	No attendance required
STARTING DATE	Fixed annual starting date	Limited number of starting dates	Wide choice of starting dates	Start any time
ASSESSMENT METHODS	Externally fixed method of assessment; no negotiation	Some choice available as to method but only in special cases	Learner chooses between wide range of assessment activity	Learner constructs methods of demonstrating competence

See Section Seven for a fuller development of this approach.

Activity

First adapt the framework (questions, aspects and continuum) to suit your own scheme, ie:

— decide which questions you wish to examine and name them
— decide which aspects you wish to examine and include them on the table
— decide how you want to show openness (eg, numbered scale points).

Secondly, identify where your own scheme stands on the questions you have chosen. Thirdly, decide the following points.

— Is your scheme open to the right extent?
— Do you need to modify your scheme to make it more or less open?
— How might you do this?

The following extract shows how one institution, Holland College, developed open principles on which to operate. The college provides post-secondary education and training in Prince Edward Island, Canada. It is described in more detail in Ferguson (1982a), on which the extract is based.

> Twelve basic principles were developed and these were unanimously supported by the staff.
>
> (a) Skills required in an occupational field shall be identified by persons working in that field.
>
> (b) Credit to be given for previously acquired skills.
>
> (c) The stress to be on learning instead of teaching.
>
> (d) Students to enter or leave a programme at any time.
>
> (e) The role of the instructor shall be to assess, diagnose, prescribe and tutor but not to be the sole conveyor of information.
>
> (f) Students to be responsible for their own progress and instructors to be accountable for student progress.
>
> (g) Resource rooms, materials and instructors are scheduled and timetabled — not students.
>
> (h) Programmes shall be individualized (ie, personalized) to the full extent that resources allow.
>
> (i) Evaluation to be realistic and meaningful and in keeping with evaluation in the work environment.
>
> (j) Ratings to be based only on performance.
>
> (k) Students to evaluate their own performance prior to confirmation by an instructor.
>
> (l) Students to be able to continue their learning in a systematic way even after leaving the college.

Section Four. Advantages to Providers and Employers

Advantages to Providers and Employers

CONTENTS
Introduction
Providers of specialist training and/or employers
Schools
Further and higher education
Adult and community education

INTRODUCTION
We have shown the advantages of open learning to the recipients, whether these are called students, learners, customers, clients, trainees, or whatever. But what of the *providers* of education and training, and employers. What, if any, are the advantages to them? This section looks at the advantages open learning might have for four different kinds of provider:

— those responsible for providing specialist training, and employers
— schools
— further and higher education
— adult and community education.

There is a good deal of common ground. Here we are seeking only to highlight benefits of particular importance to each group.

Objectives
After working through this section you should be able to

— identify the main advantages open learning may have for you
— identify different kinds of advantage.

Activity
Decide which of the following four categories you fall into:

— provider of specialist training/employer (page 48)
— school (page 50)
— further and higher education (page 53)
— adult and community education (page 54).

Concentrate on whichever section is most relevant to you. Scan the others.

PROVIDERS OF SPECIALIST TRAINING AND/OR EMPLOYERS

This section lists some advantages open learning might have if you fall into this category.

Training can be started at any time. The advantage of this in the Civil Service is stressed in the following extract from *Self Instruction* (Day, 1984, pp 5–6 — see the Booklist).

> The availability, on the spot, of learning packages can make staff more versatile and ease the problems of management at a time of peak workload or sudden absence of staff through sickness. Over the years the Department of Employment has developed an extensive range of self-instructional materials on the operations involved in the payment of unemployment benefit. Initially, these were intended for casual staff recruited to work in local offices when there was a sudden upsurge in the number of unemployed. Soon afterwards they took their place in the training programme for regular staff replacing wide areas of 'Sitting next to Nellie' and substituting for a formal course. They have been used over nearly two decades and in that time they will have saved the Department very considerable sums of money. The Department is on record as saying that it would have been very hard pressed to have coped with unemployment on the present scale without this library of learning materials written in anticipation of just such an emergency. The snag about courses is that people have to wait for their training until there is a big enough batch to make a course worthwhile. The snag about 'Sitting next to Nellie' is that she must be free to carry out the training and not so embroiled in urgent work as to make this impossible. In any case, there is nothing more motivating than getting the training just when it's needed and there's nothing better for the reputation of a training organisation than making this possible.

Extract from 'Self Instruction' pp 5 and 6 by H Day, published by Her Majesty's Stationery Office, 1984, and reproduced by permission of the Controller of HMSO

Large numbers can be trained concurrently. The following extract is again taken from *Self Instruction* (ibid, p 5).

> Changes in procedure, perhaps stemming from new legislation or the introduction of new equipment such as a computer, can give rise to the need to impart knowledge and skills to vast numbers of people within a limited period of time. VAT, health and safety at work, new social security benefits are all examples.

Extract from 'Self Instruction', p 5, by H Day, published by Her Majesty's Stationery Office, 1984, and reproduced by permission of the Controller of HMSO

Learners of varied initial ability and readiness can be accommodated. Individuals can, after a diagnostic test, start at the appropriate point for them. This reduces training time and potential frustration. Once in the scheme, learners can then proceed at their own pace, using their own preferred style.

Training can be accommodated without employees being absent at a training centre.

The gap between 'working' and 'training' is likely to be less than is usually the case. Because training can take place on the job, the learner is more likely to relate theory to practice. Learning is linked with day-to-day working routines and it is possible to use 'real' equipment in a 'real' environment.

Per capita training cost can often be reduced by open learning (eg, travelling and subsistence costs are cut and work output is unaffected). Economies of scale apply when large numbers are trained.

The package is public and the content is identical regardless of where the learners are based. Conventional training methods are, on the other hand, very variable in standard depending on who is teaching whom, when, and on how the trainer feels on that particular day. The openness means that employers know more about the content of the training.

An open-learning package is often easy to maintain, update and amend. It is easier to update one package than a group of widely scattered trainers.

Case-study

See Zoo Animal Management; Leicester Pharmacy; YMCA; Doncaster; and Sight and Sound case-studies in Volume 1, *Open Learning in Action*.

Examples of uses of open learning in specialist training

Open learning has been used

— to ensure sales staff are fully aware of new product features and can use these as selling points
— to update staff in remote locations, eg, merchant seamen on new legislation
— to help foreign countries install, use, and maintain plant supplied from the UK
— to provide training in safety procedures to new staff as they join an organization
— to provide continuity to an employee who has been away sick
— to train staff in new methods brought about by new technology, eg, to retrain large numbers of checkout personnel to operate new equipment
— to enable senior managers to acquire new skills without incurring the personal costs of leaving their families for long periods
— to increase the range of specialist skills in staff
— to train staff who work shifts
— to train individuals after promotion or transfer.

Activity

Tick which of the above advantages apply in your case. Add any further advantages and uses relevant to you.

The following quotations give extended discussions of the advantages of open learning to providers of specialist training and employers.

> The National Federation therefore decided to adopt an open-learning approach. One very desirable feature of such a scheme would be that it could be used by a keeper in work anywhere in the country and would adjust to the market for jobs. The student could dictate the speed and direction of his learning. The framework of the course could be flexible enough to respond quickly to changes in methods of animal management.
> Open learning was particularly suitable also because this method of delivery would avoid the separation of 'education' and 'training' that often occurs in conventional courses. Learning would occur whilst the keeper was actually doing the job.
> Such a course would make demands on the student because he would have to learn without constant close supervision. But the self-management involved would pay dividends to the successful students by indicating an ability to assess a situation and deal with it independently. This ability is desirable in a zookeeper who often works alone solving day-to-day problems.

Extract from 'Zoo Animal Management Open-Learning Scheme' in 'Open Learning in Action', Open Learning Guide 1, p 73, edited by Roger Lewis and published by the Council for Educational Technology, 1984

> The course structure is completely flexible. That is to say a student may attend at times of his own choice and proceed from his current state of competence. The course of training is as long or as short as the trainee wishes it to be.

Extract from 'Sight and Sound Secretarial Training' in 'Open Learning in Action', Open Learning Guide 1, p 93, edited by Roger Lewis and published by the Council for Educational Technology, 1984

> there was also an increasing realization that structured updating was essential if pharmacists were to remain accountable both to the public and to the government. The findings of a DHSS-sponsored Pharm Soc group had highlighted this point. Relatively isolated individual pharmacists were being armed with a growing battery of potent drugs and their personal updating had become a matter of urgency.

Extract from 'The Leicester Pharmacy Project' in 'Open Learning in Action', Open Learning Guide 1, p 104, edited by Roger Lewis and published by the Council for Educational Technology, 1984

SCHOOLS

The advantages to schools and local education authorities have been very well set out by Philip Waterhouse in *Supported Self-Study in Secondary Education* (CET Working Paper 24). You should turn to that source if you work in the schools sector. The National Extension College is also working in this area (see Harding in the Booklist).

Open learning enables a school or authority to offer a broad range of subjects, choice and support; eg, it can use open learning methods to:

— maintain a small option group when it falls below a 'viable' size
— continue to teach a specialist subject when a member of staff leaves
— introduce a new subject
— provide further teaching to learners who have failed an examination and need to resit
— stretch the very able
— give the less able more chance to keep up
— meet the needs of ethnic and other minority groups
— provide support courses to the main timetabled subjects, eg, in study skills, numeracy, information technology
— offer enrichment courses, eg, in ecology, computer appreciation
— lessen the effect of timetable clashes
— cater for different ability levels within a class or group
— help a learner ill or in hospital to maintain progress
— enable learners to pursue interests not represented on the timetable
— help a learner who joins the school mid-term from another area
— help learners being taught elsewhere, by supporting their studies and providing continuity (eg, allowing contact to be maintained with a known and trusted member of staff who may act as a counsellor)
— cater for learners who dislike working in a group and who prefer to work on their own
— provide an alternative for learners who have rejected conventional teaching methods
— allow self-pacing, so the learner can use his time in relation to his needs and interests.

The numbers involved in any one of the above may be small but the use of open learning enables a wide range of such needs to be met. Once a package is used for any of the above purposes teachers can then use it for other purposes, without having to acquire any further skills. Open learning helps teachers:

— to take on an unfamiliar subject or age group
— to help learners to acquire greater autonomy
— to help learners to develop as individuals
— to foster better staff–student personal relationships
— to help students to learn.

Open learning:

— provides a more satisfying and productive role for the teacher
— frees the teacher from information-giving and thus makes it possible to give more personal support, guidance and consultancy to the learner
— helps teachers to acquire new skills, sharpen existing skills and thus improve their mainstream work.

52 WHAT IS OPEN LEARNING?

The comments in HMI reports on schools suggest a role for open-learning methods, as the following extracts show:

> Many reports ... include adverse comments on teaching styles. The main concerns are that there is too much teacher direction and not enough involvement of pupils in their learning, and that pupils at all levels of ability are not being sufficiently challenged. Particular references include: success being achieved only within narrow objectives; pupils being too dependent on teacher input; teacher and pupil expectations that are too low; narrowly conceived and executed work; lack of pace; and neglect of oral work ...
>
> attention should be given to the spreading and sharing of good practice throughout a school, to the development of teaching styles which take more account of individual abilities, to the improvement of continuity and progression, to giving pupils more responsibility for their own learning, to placing more emphasis on oral work and discussion, and to relating the work more closely to pupils' own experience and interests. Self-evaluation by schools may be a helpful way forward in the future; so far only a minority of schools have made effective use of this procedure ...

Extract from 'Education Observed', p 6, by HM Inspectors, published by the Department of Education and Science, 1984, and reproduced by permission of the Controller of Her Majesty's Stationery Office

> In fourth and fifth year classes especially, much of the teaching and learning is narrowly focussed on what teachers perceive, sometimes wrongly, to be the requirements of public examinations. As a consequence, approaches to work in the classroom are often assiduous but over-cautious. Pupils need to be encouraged, and expected, to take more responsibility for their work.
>
> the need for teachers to have higher expectations of their pupils, to take greater account of pupils' individual differences and generally to make lessons less 'teacher-dominated':

Extract from 'Education Observed 2', pp 8 and 12, by HM Inspectors, published by the Department of Education and Science, 1984, and reproduced by permission of the Controller of Her Majesty's Stationery Office

Activity
If you work in a school, decide which of the above advantages are of most importance.

Case-study

> Clwyd LEA first showed an active interest in the idea of distance learning in schools in 1977–78. There were many reasons for this interest. A significant one was an awareness of the growth of the 'new sixth form' with more pupils returning to school for a sixth and seventh year of full-time education without, however, either wishing to pursue — or being necessarily suited to — the traditional three A-level 'academic' sixth-form course. At the same time there was a growing interest in subjects previously not widely studied in schools, such as sociology and psychology. It was felt that it would be difficult to support the offer of extra subjects in the sixth form to groups of pupils that would probably be small (and uneconomic to staff with specialists) at a time of cutbacks in the education service. There was an awareness within the authority of developments in the field of open learning in further education, so it was decided to investigate open learning's possible application in schools.

Extract from 'Clwyd Local Education Authority Distance-Learning Scheme' in 'Open Learning in Action', Open Learning Guide 1, p 176, edited by Roger Lewis and published by the Council for Educational Technology, 1984

FURTHER AND HIGHER EDUCATION

The very wide variety of programmes of education and training that characterize the typical institution of further/higher education make open learning particularly beneficial to them. If you work in this sector you can readily identify, in the other sections, advantages that apply to you too. For those providing mainly vocational training, the advantages are akin to those listed for providers of specialist training and employers. Those in more general education have benefits similar to those working in schools.

Activity

Read through the lists of advantages given for

— providers of specialist training/employers
— schools.

Add any advantages which are particularly important to you.

Here are some additional advantages which you may have noted.

Open learning enables a college to provide courses for learners who might not come together in sufficient numbers during conventional enrolment periods. In September, for example, 12 people may want to study O-level English and this may not be enough to run the class. But over the year the total numbers wishing to study the subject may be 50–100. Open learning enables the college to meet the needs of this group.

Open learning makes it easier for management to monitor the performance of individual learners.

Open learning enables a college to meet the needs of a scattered rural population for whom regular attendance is impossible.

Colleges can extend their role in adult or community education through outreach. Modular open-learning materials mean that students on different syllabuses, possibly working towards accreditation by a number of boards, can be accommodated — in a single class if necessary.

Packaged materials, once prepared, can be used by other courses and exchanged with other colleges. Also, colleges can make use of materials produced under the Open Tech and similar programmes.

Case-study

See the Peterborough, Luton, and Telford case-studies in Volume 1, *Open Learning in Action*. See, too, the accounts in *Flexible Learning in Action* (see Birch and Latcham, 1984a, in the Booklist).

In East Anglia distances are relatively large, public transport is poor and the number of students in many specialized fields of study is low; here open learning is the only workable solution to a number of problems.

East Anglia is one of the most productive sugar beet regions in the country and so has a large number of sugar factories, including a very large plant at Peterborough. The work is very seasonal with a period of frantic activity known as 'the campaign' which starts in October and runs through to February. During this time the factory runs 24 hours a day, seven days a week, and staff just about have time to eat and sleep; study is not possible. The College therefore runs the accountancy course on an open-learning basis.

Extract from 'Open Learning at Peterborough Technical College' in 'Open Learning in Action', Open Learning Guide 1, pp 236–7, edited by Roger Lewis and published by the Council for Educational Technology, 1984

ADULT AND COMMUNITY EDUCATION

If you work in this sector you can readily identify, in the other sections, advantages that apply to you too.

Activity

Read quickly through the advantages listed earlier, ie, those for providers of specialist training and/or employers and for schools and colleges. Tick which of the advantages also apply to you. Write down any further advantages of open learning in your sector.

ADVANTAGES TO PROVIDERS AND EMPLOYERS 55

You may have noted some of the following.
Open learning helps people, both individuals and groups, to help themselves.
Open learning materials can be targeted very precisely on a particular group.
The philosophy behind open learning, in particular its stress on autonomy and on meeting the needs of individuals, is shared by many adult educators.

Case-study

These advantages are well expressed in the case-studies of the BBC Computer Literacy Project and the Open University Health Education Programme.

> A massive job of public education in the implications of the microchip revolution was needed... 7,000,000 people watched *The Computer Programme*, 8,000,000 *Making the Most of the Micro*; 85,000 copies of *The Computer Book* were sold, 250,000 BBC microcomputers, 120,000 copies of *30-Hour BASIC*, 50,000 students went to classes...

Figures quoted in the 'BBC Computer Literacy Project 1979–83' in 'Open Learning in Action', Open Learning Guide 1, edited by Roger Lewis and published by the Council for Educational Technology, 1984

> The primary aim was to help people make and implement practical decisions affecting their daily lives... it was felt essential to collaborate with other organizations - (those with) a base in the local community (and) a 'grassroots' network... the spontaneous development of external initiatives in using the course materials 'informally' far surpassed the expectations of the course teams... Most of the women taking part (in Glasgow) have previously been non participants in adult education or community affairs.

Aims quoted in 'The Open University Health Education Programme' in 'Open Learning in Action', Open Learning Guide 1, edited by Roger Lewis and published by the Council for Educational Technology, 1984

Quiz

List two or three advantages that are both common and important to all four categories of provider discussed in this section.

Answer
You may have listed some of the following:
— consistent education/training standards
— education/training can be started at any time
— individual needs can be met
— small numbers can be dealt with easily
— teacher/trainer time can be given to counselling and small-group work
— autonomy can be promoted.

Section Five. Staff Development and the Open Learning Guides

Staff Development and the Open Learning Guides

CONTENTS
Introduction
The challenge of open learning
New roles for staff in open learning
Staff development in open learning
Using the Guides

INTRODUCTION
Open learning brings changes of role for staff, whether they are in education or training. The first part of this section describes various new roles staff may need to play. The second part spells out some of these roles more fully. These roles are not limited to open learning — they are also needed in other current developments in education and training.

Given the changes in role, staff development becomes very important. What activities will staff carry out in an open-learning scheme? What skills will they need to acquire? Finally, how can the Guides series help, and what other resources are available for staff development?

Objectives
After working through this section you should be able to

— list the activities staff will need to carry out in your open-learning scheme
— identify some major new roles for staff in open-learning schemes
— explain the implications of open-learning for staff other than teachers and trainers
— use the Open Learning Guides and other resources as training aids for staff in your scheme.

THE CHALLENGE OF OPEN LEARNING
When open learning is first mentioned staff, whether in industry or training, sometimes feel alarmed.

> the scheme began there was a good deal of doubt and suspicion about the approach. The uncertainties included:
> — the belief that open learning would reduce the number of students on full-time courses
> — the feeling that open learning was asking too much of lecturers in terms of time
> — the conviction that only the interaction between lecturers and students in the classroom could be a successful method of teaching.

Extract from 'Telford College of Further Education Flexistudy Courses' in 'Open Learning in Action', Open Learning Guide 1, p 54, edited by Roger Lewis and published by the Council for Educational Technology, 1984

These fears can be intensified if new technology is involved. The Coventry Computer-Based Learning Project describes these fears: 'A few staff showed concern at an early stage in the project that PLATO would mean a reduction in their professional workload. This was found not to be the case although *the use of CBI does change roles; staff spend more time in helping individual students follow personal learning programmes and in picking up and dealing with problems detected in class or group teaching'* (original emphasis) (CBI: computer based instruction, Lister, para 6.46).

This extract points out that staff are still needed, but to carry out different roles.

Activity

Look at the job description of the lecturer given the task of managing the Bradford Maths Workshop, reprinted below. Tick tasks which go beyond straight 'lecturing'.

> My job description involved the following tasks:
>
> — oversee the general development of a working area in the College devoted to the study and learning of mathematics
> — develop students notes, workcards, learning packages and review lessons and also provide a collection of textbooks and past examination papers with solutions
> — be responsible for obtaining, maintaining and updating a collection of pocket electronic calculators for use of students and staff
> — supervise the computing facilities within the Mathematics Workshop
> — index and catalogue all learning materials in the Workshop
> — direct and supervise staff allocated to assist in the Workshop
> — be aware of new developments and incorporate educationally sound ideas into the Workshop, for example, computer-assisted learning
> — test all first-year students entering College with a Mathematics Survey Test as required

STAFF DEVELOPMENT AND THE OPEN LEARNING GUIDES 61

> — make the Workshop a base where anyone might attend to achieve basic numeracy
> — assist with the development of mathematics, either as a course, or within courses throughout the College
> — provide a tutorial service in mathematics for students needing help at any level
> — assist with the implementation of computer-assisted management of learning in mathematics
> — provide resources for lecturers requiring background material and teaching materials for mathematics classes
> — provide facilities for the preparation of mathematical models and teaching aids.

Extract from 'The Bradford Mathematics Workshop' in 'Open Learning in Action', Open Learning Guide 1, p 141, edited by Roger Lewis and published by the Council for Educational Technology, 1984

The change in role is summarized in Volume 3, *How to Tutor and Support Learners*, as follows.

Customary	*New*
Performance in a classroom.	Little or no chance to perform.
A group of learners is addressed.	An individual is addressed.
Face-to-face teaching.	Distance/mediated learning.
Choice of subject matter and the way it is structured.	Content is preselected and pre-structured by the package writer.
Subject orientation.	General support orientation/ learning consultant.
Ad hoc marking, relying on face-to-face contact with the learner.	Elaborated marking to communicate across a distance.
Potential for easy and regular learner contact.	Contact with learner brief, intermittent and hard to schedule.
Tendency to wait for learner to take initiative, eg, to declare a 'problem'.	Tendency to intervene in advance of the learner experiencing a problem.

Extract from 'How to Tutor and Support Learners', Open Learning Guide 3, p 62, by Roger Lewis and published by the Council for Educational Technology, 1984

The new roles extend to many new curriculum initiatives: 'The incorporation of pupil *learning strategies* such as experiential learning, participation/negotiation and community involvement encourages pupils to internalise and apply their learning, take responsibility for it, and recognise a variety of experiences as part of it. This carries with it a change in teachers' role to become not so much knowledge providers but facilitators of learning and reflectors of the pupils' processes of decision making,' (*Progressing to College: a 14–16 core,* Further Education Unit, 1985, pp 6-7).

The next part of this section explores in more detail what these new or additional roles involve.

NEW ROLES FOR STAFF IN OPEN LEARNING

The individual member of staff may be called upon to play one or more new roles. Here we explore a few of those most frequently met: coordinator, facilitator, curriculum designer, materials developer and team member.

Coordinator

Coordination can be complex, involving such activities as keeping track of learners following individual programmes of study, and the delivery and despatch of learning materials. Some activities may seem routine. The Coventry Computer-Based Learning Project reports the crucial role played by coordinators (called learning centre administrators). These key people had to be versatile and capable of dealing with:

— technical problems
— simple equipment maintenance
— evaluation of software
— simple programming
— record-keeping
— the maintenance of an efficient booking system.

(See too the job description of the Bradford Maths Workshop manager on pp 60–61.)

The learning centre administrators were a source of support both directly to the learner and also to the tutors whose students used the learning centres. They gave advice on how to get the most from the system. Where a centre lacked such a coordinator several ill effects were noted, eg:

— liaison with tutors was poor
— usage was patchier and less consistent than in centres with coordinators.
— integration of the package with other aspects of the learner's course suffered
— fewer people used the packages
— records were unreliable.

Case-study

The case-studies in Volume 1, *Open Learning in Action,* show the need for a similar versatility on the part of tutor and others involved in open-learning schemes. See particularly the studies of Telford, Zoo Animal Management, Sight and Sound, the Bradford Mathematics Workshop, Dundee, Clwyd and Luton.

> *The personal tutor*
> From the start we felt that adequate counselling and supervision of each pupil's progress were important because
>
> — the pupils are aged only 16+ when they begin the course
> — they need encouragement and advice to help them adjust to this new method of studying
> — the open-learning method implies a measure of independence, self-discipline and motivation which the average pupil *can* achieve gradually given adequate sympathy and support.
>
> So, it is a condition of a school's participation in the scheme that it appoints a member of staff to act as personal tutor to the pupils of that school. The selection is entirely a matter for the headteacher of the school. The personal tutor's time allocation with the pupils is also entirely a matter for the school but most have two periods a week with each group. His roles fall into two broad categories — pastoral and administrative.
>
> *Pastoral duties.* These include advice and guidance with problems of a personal nature, and help with problems of a study skills nature. No knowledge of sociology is assumed. The most important factor is that the teacher knows the learner as an individual and is aware of his strengths and weaknesses, while the learner is reassured by the interest and support of a teacher whom he knows and trusts.
>
> *Administrative duties.* The personal tutor is a vital link between the learners in the schools and the NEWI and the tutors. The package of sociology learning materials arrives weekly at each school, addressed to the personal tutor. The units are distributed to the pupils and the completed assignments are collected and sent to the course tutor to be marked. The personal tutor liaises with the course tutor over tutorial assignments; he is responsible for recording assignment grades on a record card (see page 180) and also arranges for pupils to use audio-visual learning materials when these form part of the unit being studied.

Extract from 'Clwyd Local Education Authority Distance-Learning Scheme' in 'Open Learning in Action', Open Learning Guide 1, pp 178–9, edited by Roger Lewis and published by the Council for Educational Technology, 1984

Volume 5, *How to Develop and Manage an Open-Learning Scheme*, stresses the need for adequate resources for tutors to carry out their role, including the allocation of time and provision for staff development.

Facilitator
Secondly, the tutor acts as facilitator of learning. He helps the learner to formulate objectives and to plan ways of reaching these. This role is sometimes described as 'catalyst' or 'consultant' to the learner. To carry out this role the tutor needs an understanding of what learning is and how it can be brought about. He focuses not so much on the content of the learning as on the process. (See Downs and Perry in the Booklist.) The learner-centredness of open learning also elevates activities described variously as 'counselling' or 'guidance' to a major place in the tutor's repertory of

skills. The tutor may also have to relate to learners who earlier may have avoided or rejected conventional forms of provision.

Ideally our facilitator will be able to negotiate with the learner — along all the questions of the chart on pp 39–42: what will be learned? where and when? why and how? This requires diagnostic skills and the ability to use new modes of assessing learner competence. The facilitator will increasingly need to understand the principles behind, and the operation of, new assignment methods such as 'profiling'. In open learning some of these facilitating activities may be carried out across a physical distance, eg, by post or telephone or by advanced information technology.

Curriculum designer

Open learning is likely increasingly to be offered in modular form, better to suit learner and employer needs. Sequencing will be determined by negotiation and diagnostic testing (in its broadest form) rather than by traditional subject patterns or instruction for a particular occupation. The teacher will advise the learner on alternative curriculum options and adapt what exists to suit the learner. This will require a developmental approach on the part of the teacher and a commitment to meet the learner's objectives.

Materials developer

In addition to the more general capacities discussed earlier the teacher will need to acquire some specific skills. Several of these relate to materials development. The teacher may, for example, be expected to write learning material, or adapt existing material, or edit material written by colleagues. He may also need to commission or use new technologies to deliver learning — eg, computer-based training, computer management, interactive video, teleconferencing. All these are covered in the Open Learning Guides.

Team member

It will be rare for one individual to possess all the necessary skills. This means that open learning developments will usually be planned and run by teams. This will apply not only within an institution but on a wider basis — eg, the workplace or professional body will be part of the team. Tutors/trainers will thus work as team members and communicate with colleagues not only inside but also outside their institution. Open Tech schemes show both the importance of such collaboration and the difficulty of making it actually happen.

Conclusion

So the tutor's role in open learning is a demanding one. It is, however, also professionally satisfying. 'This system could not work without a high level of professional commitment by the staff implementing it. Several members of staff admitted that in the early days of the system they found it necessary to work up to 70 hours per week in preparing material and all the other multifarious things needed to get a programme started. However, they found the work very satisfying and more enjoyable than teaching in a "normal" college' (Ferguson, 1982a: the account of Holland College, see p 55).

STAFF DEVELOPMENT AND THE OPEN LEARNING GUIDES 65

Checklist
The new roles are listed below. Tick those which will be new to you and/or your colleagues.

Coordinator
Facilitator
Curriculum designer
Materials developer
Team member

STAFF DEVELOPMENT IN OPEN LEARNING
Few teachers or trainers will possess all the necessary capacities outlined above. So staff development assumes major importance. In addition, change at the moment is so rapid that constant updating is required. Professionals must be able to respond quickly to frequent changes in curriculum, assessment methods, new technologies, and new groups of learners.

When open-learning schemes are introduced it is important that relevant staff are adequately prepared. This removes some of the threat of the new, and gives ample opportunity to explain the roles staff will play. Staff can then raise in an unhurried way any misgivings they may have. They can accustom themselves to the new role they will be playing. 'Relevant' staff extend beyond teachers and trainers. Administrators, managers, and receptionists too need not only briefing but also the kind of induction that will ensure that they give the innovation their full support.

These points are reinforced in the following quotations from Volume 1, *Open Learning in Action*.

Adequate clerical staff and an adequate telephone system are both essential for open learning to work; both are regarded by many elected members as akin to original sin.

Extract from 'Open Learning at Peterborough Technical College' in 'Open Learning in Action', Open Learning Guide 1, p 241, edited by Roger Lewis and published by the Council for Educational Technology, 1984

The full-time administrative staff provide the back-up. The course administrator handles everything concerned with the operation of the course: receipts and payments, equipment ordering, maintenance of student records, organization of residential courses, despatch of materials to students.

Extract from 'The YMCA Distance-Learning Scheme' in 'Open Learning in Action', Open Learning Guide 1, p 203, edited by Roger Lewis and published by the Council for Educational Technology, 1984

> A special problem for us is overload at residential courses — every student wants 'just a few minutes'. At one residential I was 'nobbled' for an impromptu tutorial from 1.30 am to 3.30 am in the gents! The key qualities required by a distance-learning tutor are
> — an interest in the students
> — a knowledge of the circumstances in which they are endeavouring to learn
> — a sound understanding of learning processes
> — a readiness to take pains over such things as making course requirements and assessment criteria absolutely clear and unambiguous.

Extract from 'The YMCA Distance-Learning Scheme' in 'Open Learning in Action', Open Learning Guide 1, p 206, edited by Roger Lewis and published by the Council for Educational Technology, 1984

> Tutorial support is crucial in distance courses
> But, ever-conscious of the feelings of insecurity that distance learners may experience, we have tried to make even the management of the course 'personal'. Although enrolments, fees, awards of the diploma and terminations of course are controlled by the central College office, all other administrative contact with the student is via the course secretary, course organizer or tutors. The students can get to know the individuals they are dealing with. We encourage personal relationships. We use first names for students and staff. We provide students with a photograph and a tape-recording of personal details from each tutor. We give students our home telephone numbers. We add personal, friendly notes on marked assignments and standard letters. So we try to remove the impression of an impersonal, distant institution.

Extract from 'Educational Technology at a Distance from Dundee College of Education' in 'Open Learning in Action', Open Learning Guide 1, p 160, edited by Roger Lewis and published by the Council for Educational Technology, 1984

> There is always a brisk interchange of letters and telephone calls and the Unit tries to be helpful at all times. Staff other than the course leader — the school secretary, for example — are given a list of likely questions and answers for use when the Unit office is not manned. If in doubt, the rule is 'Leave an address and telephone number and we will contact you'.

Extract from 'Leicester Pharmacy Project' in 'Open Learning in Action', Open Learning Guide 1, p 106, edited by Roger Lewis and published by the Council for Educational Technology, 1984

USING THE GUIDES

How might you use the Open Learning Guides in a staff development programme? This part answers the following questions. *Who* should use the books? *Why* should they use them? *How* can the books be used? *What* is the relationship of the series to other training initiatives and services?

Who?

The series is intended for use by any of the following:
— policy-makers
— planners
— tutors
— writers
— editors
— designers
— trainers/managers interested, but not directly involved, in open learning
— students on initial and in-service courses.

Some books in the series are clearly addressed to one group: eg, Volume 7, *How to Manage the Production Process,* is primarily addressed to those responsible for managing the production of learning resources. Some books contain sections for different groups, eg, some sections of Volume 3, *How to Tutor and Support Learners,* are addressed directly to tutors, other sections to their managers.

Why?

The books may be used for a variety of different purposes. These include:
— general familiarization with open learning
— input to decisions by policy-making groups
— stimulating ideas on open-learning developments you could carry out in your own institution
— long-term planning
— detailed preparation
— answering a specific question, eg, which medium should I choose for the package? How can I find out if suitable open-learning packages exist for this subject? Who will be best placed to give learners support?
— reviewing the performance of an existing scheme, or part of it.

How?

The books are designed in open-learning form (see p 4). They can be used by an individual (for any of the purposes set out above) or by a group (eg, a planning group). You could produce extra resources, eg, assignments and self-assessment questions, to convert the series into a more formal course. The National Extension College plans to use the series along with on-the-job assignments for training its own staff.

The series could form the basis of staff development workshops or peer learning groups, or act as a catalyst in planning meetings. Individuals or groups may use the books in any way — eg:
— to read through quickly
— to read through in depth
— to carry out all the activities
— to select only the activities relevant at the time

— to use as a checklist
— to follow up examples, to see how activities were actually carried out in particular schemes
— to apply the ideas to a particular scheme
— in conjunction with existing packages such as *How to Tutor in an Open-Learning Scheme* (Lewis, 1981) or the training packages produced by the Scottish Open Tech Training Unit (SCOTTSU).

The series has been designed with all these possible ways of using the books in mind.

Other resources

Appendix One is a list of other resources and initiatives which can be used alongside the Guides.

The following extracts from Volume 1, *Open Learning in Action,*. show two approaches to staff development taken by schemes.

> The instructors are all recruited from students who have attended Sight and Sound College and are therefore familiar with the system of instruction as well as with the content of the courses. On appointment, they receive in-college training for their duties in the classes or sections. There is also an ongoing training programme to ensure that each instructor is competent in sections other than the one in which she normally works. This training involves formal sessions run by the training manager, followed by supervised working experience in the new section. Each section has a 'training pack' of notes for instructors.

Extract from 'Sight and Sound Secretarial Training' in 'Open Learning in Action', Open Learning Guide 1, p 91, edited by Roger Lewis and published by the Council for Educational Technology, 1984

> In August 1980 the Professional Tutor took up post and was also a subject tutor for the scheme. During the second year (1981–82) she coordinated a pilot scheme of workshops using the CET material *How to Tutor in an Open-Learning Scheme*. This involved two tutors in science subjects and four tutors in English meeting at intervals over five months. This proved a useful method of staff development and the results were written up in a report to CET. Since then the self-study version of *How to Tutor* has been used for part-time tutors and in-College workshops have been set up for lecturers new to the FlexiStudy scheme.
> Staff development for writing materials has also continued. In 1982 a College workshop on writing materials, funded by SCET, was arranged. Further help for individuals and for groups has been provided by the SCET Open Learning Project, the Professional Tutor and the course coordinators. With the increase in the number of tutors involved it has been possible to arrange for some tutors to work together and share the production of materials. The College now has a policy that all new tutors receive training in tutoring and in preparing materials. New tutors are attached to more experienced tutors for help and advice.

Extract from 'Telford College of Further Education Flexistudy Courses' in 'Open Learning in Action', Open Learning Guide 1, pp 54–55, edited by Roger Lewis and published by the Council for Educational Technology, 1984

Quiz

1. Below are two lists. The left-hand list summarizes some of the roles which teaching staff may have to play in an open-learning scheme. The right-hand side lists activities. Find one activity in the right-hand list for each of the roles on the left-hand side. For example, if you think that (i) is an activity of the teacher as coordinator than you match (a) with (i). (There are several alternative answers, as both the roles and the activities overlap.)

(a) coordinator

(b) facilitator

(c) curriculum designer

(d) materials developer

(i) to master an authoring language in order to prepare computer-based training materials

(ii) to help the learner find a suitable site for practical work

(iii) to advise a learner on which modules to take

(iv) to read and comment on a draft manuscript and contribute these comments to a course planning meeting

(v) to locate sources of suitable course material

(vi) to help the learner overcome a block to understanding a crucial concept

(vii) to help the learner assess his progress on a module

(viii) to advise a video producer on the content of a video

(ix) to draw up an outline of a proposed course on marketing

2. Which of the following best summarizes the intentions behind the Open Learning Guides series?

(a) the Guides, taken together, form a distance-learning course for tutors in further education and trainers in industry.

(b) The Guides are suitable, as they stand, for use in staff development workshops.

(c) The Guides are useful only for self-study.

(d) The Guides can provide a basis for training in a variety of contexts.

70 WHAT IS OPEN LEARNING?

Answers
1. There are many possible permutations, depending on the context. Here are our answers. Yours will almost certainly be different. (Note that you were asked for only one activity for each role.)
(a) and (ii). (Also, possibly, (v).)
(b) and (iii), (vi), (vii).
(c) and (iii), (ix)
(d) and (i), (iv), (v). (Also, possibly (ix).)
2. (d) is our preferred answer. Here are comments on the other options.

(a) This is mistaken on two counts. Firstly, the Guides have not been designed as a formal course. Secondly, they are planned for a very wide range of users, not simply those *directly* concerned with learners.

(b) They can be used in staff development workshops as they stand but workshop organizers will, at times, wish to provide additional material.

(c) We certainly hope the Guides will be useful for self-study. But the Guides are planned for use in other situations as well.

Section Six. The Future of Open Learning

The Future of Open Learning

CONTENTS
Introduction
A multiplicity of providers and packages
An information technology base
Autonomous and experiential learning

INTRODUCTION
In this section we forecast likely open-learning developments over the next five or so years. This will be in response to challenges such as those outlined in the following extract from *Competence and Competition* (NEDO/MSC, 1984, p 7 — see the Booklist). 'To remain competitive, British companies need to develop amongst their employees the ability to learn and the habit of learning, plus an ability to behave in a self-reliant way. More specifically, employees need to be able to:

— use acquired knowledge and skills in changing circumstances
— perform multi-task operations
— cross occupational boundaries and work in multi-occupational teams
— act in and help manage an integrated system, with an understanding of its wider purpose
— diagnose relevant problems and opportunities and take action to bring about results
— find out and acquire the knowledge and skills needed to cope with unfamiliar circumstances.'

We can identify three key features of open learning in the near future:

— an increase in the number and variety of schemes of training and education; and a similar increase in materials available for use in open learning
— an information technology base of ever-increasing power
— an increase in the value placed on autonomous learning and on experiential learning. This should affect validating bodies and the qualifications they offer.

The second of these features derives from fundamental advances in physics; the other two from the interaction of the new technology with shifts in the nature of our society. Progress is likely to be piecemeal as developments in one feature stimulate changes in another.

Objective
After working through this section you should be able to

— relate likely changes to your own situation.

74 WHAT IS OPEN LEARNING?

Activity
Decide which of the three features listed above will be most significant for you in the next five years.

A MULTIPLICITY OF PROVIDERS AND PACKAGES
Providers
For a long time there has been a sizable and growing private sector of industrial and commercial training and of more general further education. In recent years government policy has stimulated the appearance of independent providers and under the influence of the Manpower Services Commission we expect this trend to continue.

A useful survey of private provision at the time of writing (1985) can be found in Williams and Woodhall *Independent Further Education* (see the Booklist). They show that, when compared with the public sector, private provision is usually

— shorter
— more directly relevant to particular training needs
— more flexible in its timing.

'(The private sector can) provide some lessons for educational planning in the future, with respect to flexibility, the convenience and the cost advantages of short, intensive courses ... It appears likely ... that flexibility and emphasis on consumers' convenience will be factors that appear increasingly important if, as many commentators are advocating, there is to be a substantial expansion of continuing and recurrent education. In the United States the proprietary schools have established for themselves a recognised place in the spectrum of post-secondary education provision. Whether this happens in Britain also may depend on whether our system of public further education is capable of offering the same degree of adaptability and easy accessibility' (Williams and Woodhall, 1979, p 93 — see the Booklist).

Case-study
These features of private sector provision are all illustrated in the Sight and Sound case-study in Volume 1, *Open Learning in Action*.

Materials
Volume 1, *Open Learning in Action*, illustrates the range of providers of materials that are suitable for the individual learner. The providers include:

— the Open University: health education
— the BBC: computer literacy
— employers' organizations: concrete technology
— individual employers: telecommunications
— consortia: small businesses; zoo animal management
— open-learning institutions: the National Extension College's O- and A-level packages.

The Open Tech MARIS project (Materials and Resources Information Service) is revealing a very wide array of materials suitable for independent learning. These are mainly in the form of printed texts; the impact of the new information technology has yet to be felt. The numerous Open Tech projects will ensure a continued growth in the quantity and quality of learning packages.

Over the years the quality of standard textbooks has also improved greatly. Commercial publishers, notably Pan Books in its 'Breakthrough' series, are producing specially prepared learning materials. Open-learning features are thus likely to find their way increasingly into what were 'conventional' textbooks — much to the benefit of the individual learner.

The comparative ease with which good books can become the basis of more open systems is shown in the Bradford Maths Workshop case-study in Volume 1, *Open Learning in Action*.

Course material for complete courses. With the introduction of Tutor Teach in 1981 a more elaborate procedure for materials production became necessary. In Tutor Teach the programme of work for a student taking a complete maths course is based on a set textbook. The textbook is accompanied by study guides called 'units'. Each unit consists of a booklet on a topic or group of topics and contains instructions for the student to read specified parts of the textbook and work through specified exercises. Comments are provided on points of difficulty. Topics not in the textbooks are fully explained, and mistakes or misprints are corrected.

In addition to the units we also produce what we call 'student notes'. These deal with one topic, for example radian measure, and cover about six sides of A4. The topic is introduced and explained, examples are provided with worked solutions and other examples are left to the student. These notes may be taken out of the Workshop by the students.

The team of seven A-level mathematics lecturers and the Manager of the Workshop got together in May 1981 to determine the procedures for developing the required materials for a September 1981 start. The group agreed that they would not buy in prepared distance-learning packages but would use a textbook as a basis and write materials to supplement the text.

The next objective was to divide the course into 60 units of work, each intended to take a student approximately one week. By agreement each member of staff was assigned units to prepare. The procedure laid down was that after a unit had been prepared in draft form, two other staff would check it for content and style. If changes were considered necessary these would be discussed with the author, the unit would then be modified and after being checked again it would be submitted for typing. Once typed it would be returned to the author for proofreading. After proofreading the units would be sent to the College's central reprographic service who would run off an agreed number of 100.

Extract from *'The Bradford Mathematics Workshop'* in *'Open Learning in Action'*, Open Learning Guide 1, pp 150–151, edited by Roger Lewis and published by the Council for Educational Technology, 1984

76 WHAT IS OPEN LEARNING?

Activity
How will the increase in (a) providers and (b) packages affect your work?

AN INFORMATION TECHNOLOGY BASE
The facilities made possible by developments in information technology have become progressively more accessible, less expensive and more powerful. This trend will continue indefinitely. Three applications of new technology are particularly important for the future of open learning.

Firstly, individual students will be able to gain access to a great variety of computer-based learning materials. Some will use large remote databases like PRESTEL but most will use micros, either in the home or elsewhere.

Secondly, information about opportunities for training and education will be available much more widely and easily than now. Databases will be accessed by individual learners as well as by trainers, teachers, librarians and others with professional interests.

Thirdly, those managing the provision of learning will be helped by elaborate management information systems. These will give a wealth of detail about every aspect of the learner's progress, as well as more conventional financial and other management data.

Of such developments a joint CET, FEU and FESC conference paper on information and educational technology says 'All of these developments, in one way or another, will contribute towards creating a situation in which the learner can, if he so wishes, take a large measure of control over what he learns and when and how he learns it', 'Information technology and educational development', CET/FEU/FESC Conference Paper, 1984 (see the Booklist).

Activity
How are developments in information technology likely to affect you and your learners in the near future?

AUTONOMOUS AND EXPERIENTIAL LEARNING
Autonomy within formal frameworks of training and education
To give the learner freedom of choice as to what, where, when and how has been the central aim of open systems all along. Earlier in this volume, especially in Sections Two and Three, we have surveyed some of the ways that barriers have been overcome and openness increased. This is taken further in the discussion of learner flexibility profiles in Section Seven. Those profiles relate to learner autonomy within an institutional framework, as in a college or training centre. Experiential learning, in contrast, is usually understood to occur outside such a framework.

Life experience and learning
These days most of us learn a great deal from papers, journals and books as well as from radio and television. Our learning may be casual in every sense or it may be more structured as in the case-studies related in Volume 1, *Open Learning in Action*

(Open University Health Education, BBC Computer Literacy Project, Small Businessmen). We may learn even more from talking and working with others with similar occupations or interests.

Our present systems of training and education largely ignore this 'unsponsored' acquisition of skills and knowledge. It is as if there are two worlds. The first 'formal' training and education, where you are given 'tickets' which certify that you have learned something (precisely what may not be at all clear). The second is 'life', where you may acquire important and extensive capabilities, but these can never be given formal recognition.

In *The Knowledge Revolution* (see Booklist), Norman Evans sees the marrying of these two worlds as the essential key that opens the way to an infinitely flexible future.

Anyone devising an 'open' system should give due weight to previous experiential learning in the methods of assessment, both on entry to the programme and at the end of it. Equally, opportunities for experiential learning within the programme itself should be thoughtfully exploited.

Entry procedure
Most courses allow discretion as to the prior knowledge or skill of those who may be admitted. This discretion is not always exercised. Often one of the inhibiting factors is the lack of an 'agreed procedure' for giving credit. Actual tests are rarely used outside mathematics and it is usually left to the judgement of individual admissions tutors or boards.

Learning arrangements
Many programmes such as YTS (the Youth Training Scheme) place great importance on work experience, fieldwork, practical projects and similar activities. Such activities are recognized as having important experiential elements. We believe they will increasingly be seen as part of the movement to more open systems. The YMCA case-study in Volume 1, *Open Learning in Action*, illustrates a conscious use of experiential learning by including exercises 'For you to do' which involve actual fieldwork or which draw directly on the learner's work experiences.

Final assessment
The ultimate open system would be one where you and I could present ourselves, explain that we had somehow acquired certain skills and knowledge and inquire what our 'unsponsored' learning was worth in terms of recognized training or educational qualifications. We are certainly a long way from that, though Business and Technician Education Council regulations allow students to be excused some units if they can demonstrate the required competence.

Any 'open' scheme where there is an award of any sort should ensure that its final assessment arrangements can give full credit for any earlier experiential learning.

In future we expect adults to be able to shop around for a scheme that most adequately recognizes the value of their skills and knowledge, however acquired.

Structure of qualifications
It is now very clear that modular schemes provide the best basis for open systems. Modules allow learners significant choice of what to learn, and enable credit to be given and transferred.

Oxford Polytechnic has been running a modular course since 1973 and the case for modularity in open-learning systems is well made in a single paragraph in David Watson's 'The Oxford Polytechnic Modular Course 1973–83' in the *Journal for Higher Education*, 9, 1, Spring 1985.

> The reasons for the Polytechnic's heavy investment in this programme are simple: cost effectiveness has been allied with a perceived need for more flexible and responsive approach to course design. As a result of economies of scale (especially in the delivery of basic instruction in a series of widely applicable subject areas such as accounting, computing, law, mathematics, statistics and graphic design), as well as the central administration of the affairs of a large body of students with a wide variety of intended awards, the Course has anticipated several features favoured in the current debate. These include: provision for intermediate awards; the opportunity to change or redirect rather than abandon academic study; widespread use of credit transfer; the opportunity to pick up parts of a specialised course for career enchancement, updating of skills, or for personal satisfaction; and the availability of all parts of the Course on an undifferentiated full-time, part-time or mixed-mode basis.

Extract from 'The Oxford Polytechnic Modular Course 1973–83' in the 'Journal of Higher Education', 9, 1, 1985, p 12, reproduced by permission of the editor

In CET Working Paper 19 (1980), the following was said.

> In an ideal open system of further education there would be a single (or at least, a coherent) structure of awards. There are moves in this direction in higher education with the proposed establishment of a national information service on credit transfer while the Open University gives credits for all previous relevant learning. The fractured and incompatible award structures that characterize further education are a serious source of frustration to the individual who crosses conventional educational boundaries and a consequent waste of talent to the nation.

Extract from 'Thinking About Open Learning Systems', Working Paper 19, p 51, by D C Spencer and published by the Council for Educational Technology, 1980

In 1985 we cannot report much progress in England and Wales. But for 16–18-year-olds in Scotland there is an 'Action Plan'. Three quotations from the *Guide for Parents and Students* (see the Booklist) will make our points for us.

THE FUTURE OF OPEN LEARNING 79

> This autumn new educational opportunities will be available for students in Scottish colleges of further education and the senior levels of secondary schools. A framework of new courses, based on modules or short units of study, will lead to the award of a single new National Certificate. This will replace the present profusion of courses and certificates issued by such bodies as the Scottish Business Educational Council (SCOTBEC) and the Scottish Technical Education Council (SCOTEC) and make available wider opportunities for students and employers.
>
> The Government's programme to introduce this new framework — known as the Action Plan — is of great importance for all young people who have reached or will be reaching school leaving age. The new courses will fit in better with student needs and interests and the requirements of employers for recruitment and training.
>
> ## ADVANTAGES OF THE NEW SYSTEM
>
> The new system will offer important advantages to students:
>
> **Motivation** will be improved because modules can be assembled into programmes which are better suited to the needs of individuals and their employers;
>
> **Flexibility** because modules are relatively short and successful completion of each can be recorded separately on the new National Certificate;
>
> **Choice** because the new programmes will cover a wide range of topics and bring in students in colleges, jobs, training schemes or secondary schools as well as people returning to education later on.
>
> ### What exactly is a module?
>
> A module is a unit of study and learning lasting usually for 40 hours. Everything in the module is explained in advance, including what students are expected to learn, i.e. the 'learning outcomes'. There will be tests to see if students have mastered them.
>
> ### What kind of tests?
>
> There may be some short written tests. But teachers and lecturers will be constantly monitoring the students' work to gauge how well they are doing and to provide help. Many of the tests will be practical to give students the opportunity to show what they have learned.

Extract from '16–18s in Scotland. An Action Plan. Guide for Parents and Students', published by the Scottish Education Department, 1984, and reproduced by permission of the Controller of Her Majesty's Stationery Office (this material has since been revised)

This is the basis for a truly open system for adults as well as young people.

A | **Activity**
In your present situation what are the arrangements for giving credit for experiential learning?

Section Seven. Job Aids

Job Aids

CONTENTS
Introduction
Learner flexibility profiles
Staff development profiles
An open learning toolkit

INTRODUCTION
In this section we draw attention to three aids particularly valuable to those developing open systems. They are
— learner flexibility profiles
— staff development profiles
— an open learning toolkit.

O | **Objectives**
After working through this section you should be able to
— use learner flexibility profiles to extend the openness of your scheme
— plan a staff development programme for open learning
— use the open learning toolkit to draw up plans of action for developing your scheme.

LEARNER FLEXIBILITY PROFILES
Section Three suggested ways of assessing where a particular scheme is open and where it is closed. It also showed a way of scoring openness. This part of the Job Aids section takes this approach further, for readers who need more detail.
'Learner flexibility profiles' provide a means of gaining insight into the nature and extent of the discretion of choices available to learners. In Coombe Lodge Working Paper No. 1612 (see the Booklist), Latcham and Spencer give a detailed account of how to devise and use such profiles. The document is intended for use in institutions of further and higher education but you can readily adapt it to analyse the degrees of autonomy given to learners based elsewhere, for example in industry or in schools.
To produce a profile you need a simple scale to indicate the degree of discretion given to the learner. Latcham and Spencer suggest using four-point scales. Examples are shown below (the list is adapted from Appendix A of Coombe Lodge Working Paper No. 1612).

Aspect	Scale of openness
Content, aims and objectives	1. No choice 2. Narrow choice inside specified curriculum 3. Wide choice inside specified curriculum 4. Negotiable outside specified curriculum
Entry requirements	1. Rigid pattern of formal qualifications 2. Flexible range of formal qualifications 3. Evidence of maturity and appropriate experience 4. None
Learning methods	1. Formal classes, closely defined practical activities 2. Formal activities supplemented by flexible tutorials and seminars 3. Some formal classes but wide range of informal activities 4. 'Open-ended' practical, project and other activity
Learning resources	1. Only resources are notes taken in class 2. Handouts and/or textbook references 3. Learning packages of print material 4. Packages supplemented by 'technology'
Access to tutorial support	1. Correspondence support only 2. Access in person or by telephone at planned times 3. Planned meetings with flexible access by telephone 4. Flexible access in person or by telephone
Practical activities	1. None 2. Normal laboratory or workshop activities 3. Flexible laboratory or workshop 4. Practical activities out of college
Work experience	1. None 2. Some within college simulations 3. Some short work placements 4. Ample work placements
Group work	1. None 2. Little group work under close teacher control 3. Frequent loosely structured group work with ready access to teachers 4. Much group work with little teacher intervention

Starting date	1. Fixed 2. Narrow choice 3. Wide choice 4. Free choice
Finishing date	1. Fixed 2. Limited choice of assessment date 3. Wide choice of assessment date 4. Free choice
Attendance pattern	1. Weekly or more frequent meetings 2. Occasional group meetings 3. Individual meetings with tutors 4. None
Assessment pattern	1. Annual 2. Several times per year 3. On demand 4. None
Assessment methods	1. Fixed patterns of conventional examinations and tests 2. Limited choice of standard methods 3. Wide choice of standard methods 4. Negotiable 'demonstrations of achievement'

Location of constraints

Perhaps the most striking use of learner flexibility profiles is as a device for identifying, in the administrative framework, the points at which the learner's autonomy is restricted.

The typical administrative framework of further and higher education may be presented as shown in the figure below.

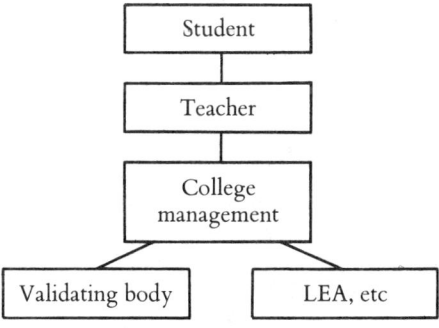

Within such a framework Latcham and Spencer provide three examples (overleaf).

Example	Dimension	Level	Student	Teacher	Management	Central body
1	Pace	Programme	1	1	1*	4
2	Learning methods	Unit A	4	4	4	4
		Unit B	1	1*	4	4
		Unit C	2	2*	4	4
3	Curriculum content	Programme	2	2	2*	3
		Unit A	2	2	2	2*
		Unit B	1	1*	2	2
		Unit C	2	2	2	2*

* Indicates points of constraint

(*Note:* 'Programme' refers to the course of study as a whole; a 'unit' is one part of the course of study. Thus a 'programme' comprises a number of 'units'.)

Example 1. Pace
Here the central body imposes no strict timetable and allows assessment to be carried out as required. The college management, however, decides not to take advantage of the flexibility available and works strictly to the pattern of the college year. Under these conditions there is no choice available to teachers or students.

Example 2. Learning methods
Here the central body allows total flexibility in choice of learning method and the college management has made appropriate support facilities available. Only one of the three teachers (Unit A) is making full use of the full variety of learning methods. Unit B is being taught conventionally while the teacher of Unit C is less conventional but still some way from taking full advantage of the freedom offered.

Example 3. Curriculum content
This example illustrates the case where the central body allows for significant choice at programme level through the variety of options which are available. The college, however, may have been unable to recruit sufficient students to justify a full range of options. Within each of the constituent units the central body offers only a limited choice of objectives and although the student has choice within Units A and C the teacher of Unit B has not found it possible to make the full choice available.

A | **Activity**
1. Identify a group of learners of interest to you.

2. Identify one or more aspects either from those given on pp 84–85 or devised by yourself.

3. Decide what features you think characterize each of the four scale points, using the system set out on pp 83–85, or one of your own. (Note that you can use more than four points if you wish.)

4. Which scale point are your chosen learners on?

5. If they are not already on the highest point, ie, enjoying maximum autonomy, then work upwards through the administrative framework, using the illustration on p 85 as a guide, until you can say who or what is limiting their freedom of choice.

6. Consider what you can do to widen learner choice at this point.

STAFF DEVELOPMENT PROFILES

The FEU publication, *Teaching Skills* (see the Booklist), is subtitled *Towards a strategy of staff development and support for vocational preparation*. So similar are the demands made on staff by vocational preparation and open learning that we think the whole of this publication will be of great interest to many readers.

Section Three of *Teaching Skills* is entitled 'Identifying and assessing the needs of teaching staff in response to vocational preparation'. The questions it asks, together with the subsequent profiling, form an excellent basis for reviewing the needs of staff involved in open learning.

Relevant parts of the section are reproduced below.

TO WHAT EXTENT ARE STAFF CONFIDENT . . . ?

1. A Student Centred Approach
 that they have had successful experience of student-centred curriculum:

 by teaching within a flexible curriculum framework which seeks to integrate different subject and/or vocational studies;

 by negotiating with the learners an approach which seeks to work from their perceived and/or identified needs; and both recognises and acts upon feedback from them;

 by supporting learners with counselling and guidance;

by providing learners with formative as well as summative assessment in a systematic way, perhaps through the operation of checklists, student profiles and/or appraisals; and

by providing relevant and appropriate learning experiences.

2. *Curriculum Innovation*
   that they are able to introduce curriculum innovation:

   by acquiring relevant information about new curricula;

   by disseminating information on new curricula among other tutors;

   by interpreting aims and objectives and devising schemes or work to implement them;

   by responding to the requirement of different teaching and learning arrangements;

   by encouraging and assisting others to respond to new curricula; and

   by persuading decision-makers and/or decision-making bodies to accept new curricula.

3. *Method Innovation*
   that they are able to use new teaching/learning methods:

   by acquiring relevant information on and experience of new methods;

   by disseminating information on new methods among other agencies;

   by working with other tutors in adapting and devising new methods;

   by judging the appropriateness of various methods of the requirements of a particular curriculum and the needs of those learners;

by using new methods such as games, simulations, role-play, group work of various kinds and residential periods;* and

by attempting to evaluate the effectiveness of methods.

4. *Team Coordination*
   that they are able to coordinate activities within a team:

   by managing a group concerned with curriculum planning, teacher/learning methods, resources and similar activities through leadership and/or membership of that group;

   by enabling all members to fully contribute and overcoming the interpersonal difficulties associated with this;

   by achieving progress and making decisions; and

   by effectively communicating the teams's views and decisions to other individuals and/or groups.

5. *Team Membership*
   that they have had successful experience of team membership:

   by accepting the operational patterns of a team or working party;

   by making effective contributions to its work;

   by accepting and responding to the contributions made by others; and

   by fulfilling the tasks allocated to or taken on by the team, within the constraints of time and resources.

6. *Liaison and Negotiation*
   that they are able to liaise and negotiate:

   with young people as clients;

with sponsoring and resource-providing agencies such as ITBs, LEAs, research agencies, charitable foundations;

with employers and other agencies for the provision of work experience, visits and similar experience;

with colleagues and other members of the institution for the allocation of facilities and resources; and

with assessors and moderators.

7. *Basic Skills Teaching*
that they are able to teach basic skills*:

by understanding the concept of a common core checklist of skills and the way in which it has to be further developed to include a local dimension relating to the needs of individual students;

by an awareness of their own expertise and knowledge in the areas of the common core;

by an awareness of the relationships between the areas of the common core and vocational studies;

by appreciating the need to teach common core skills through vocational topics and *vice versa;* and

by appreciating the concept of generic skills and the problems of teaching for transferability and progression.

Analysis of Staff Needs and the Initiation of a Staff Development Programme

41. Whatever the method used to identify staff needs from curriculum demands (whether through questioning or the use of any of the methods outlined in Appendix VI), some sort of analysis is necessary before a staff development programmer can be initiated. It is possible to

represent the results as a STAFF DEVELOPMENT PROFILE, which for an individual member of staff might appear as follows:—

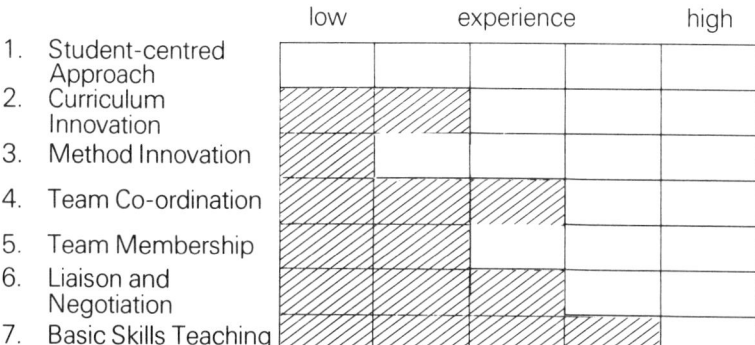

1. Student-centred Approach
2. Curriculum Innovation
3. Method Innovation
4. Team Co-ordination
5. Team Membership
6. Liaison and Negotiation
7. Basic Skills Teaching

Figure 1. A Staff Development Profile for an Individual Member of Staff

This member of staff, whilst having no previous experience of a student-centred approach, had previously been involved in the introduction of new curricular under TEC, initially as a member of a small working party and latterly as a course tutor. His role as course tutor, though taken on very recently, had required liaison and negotiation, both internally with other sections of his own department and externally with a number of local employers. He is also a competent specialist vocational teacher and would have no difficulty, for example, in teaching to Aims 1, 3, 6, 8, 10 and 11 of the core skills checklist.*

* See Appendix VII and FEU. *Vocational Preparation* 1981 Appendix VIII or *ABC In Action* Appendix III.

Extract from 'Teaching Skills: towards a strategy of staff development and support for vocational preparation', published by the Further Education Unit, 1982, and reproduced by permission of the Unit

You are referred to *Teaching Skills* for further detail, including a useful discussion of how a staff development profile can be developed for a team of tutors as well as for an individual.

AN OPEN LEARNING TOOLKIT

This job aid for managers of open-learning schemes has been produced by the National Extension College for the Trainer Development Section of the Manpower Services Commission. The toolkit identifies the key skills and key activities needed in planning and setting up an open-learning scheme. Then, by using action plans and other staged procedures, it provides a formal basis for the management of open-learning schemes.

Key skills

The Open Learning Toolkit (see pp 93–94) lists 29 main skills that are required. The word 'skills' is treated in the broadest sense to include necessary knowledge and attitudes. The list includes the skills generally agreed to be important, without claiming to be comprehensive. The skills are grouped under the headings 'managing', 'supporting learners' and 'preparing/producing packages'.

In the *Toolkit* the list is followed by a six-stage procedure intended to ensure that the manager of the open-learning scheme will have the necessary skills available when needed.

The skills list, and the six-stage procedure, are reproduced below.

Preparing and producing learning packages

analysing need ☐

writing objectives ☐

writing interactive features (e.g. self-assessment
   questions and activities) and feedback ☐

adapting existing packages ☐

selecting media ☐

authoring ☐

editing ☐

designing ☐

producing ☐

delivering ☐

Managing

team building ⟹ recruiting / allocating roles / delegating / coaching / leading ☐

marketing ☐

decision-making ☐

liaising ☐

planning ⟹ scheduling / financial planning ☐

organising ☐

prioritising ☐

supervising ☐

monitoring ☐

diagnosing where and when help is required ☐

piloting ☐

validating ☐

evaluating ☐

modifying and updating the scheme ☐

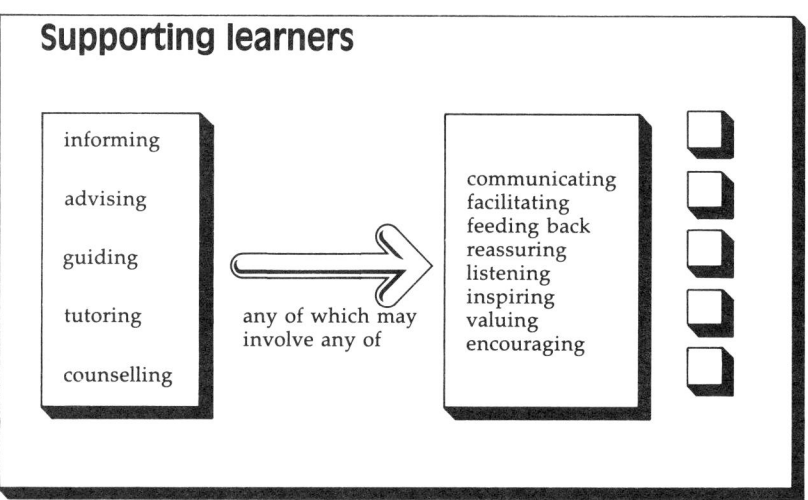

Extracts from 'The Open Learning Toolkit', published by the National Extension College on behalf of the Manpower Services Commission, 1985, and reproduced by permission of the College (Crown copyright 1985)

Activity

We have designed the activity that follows to enable you to make the best possible use of the chart in your own situation.

Stage 1 If necessary, add to, or otherwise amend the above list to suit your circumstances. You are then left with a list of the skills your project needs.

Stage 2 Tick off those skills already embodied in your team.

Stage 3 Look at those skills that are left. There are three routes you may take:
- Appoint new staff (A)
- Train existing staff (T)
- Buy in from outside, e.g. on a consultancy basis (C)

Mark each skill A, T or C as appropriate.

Stage 4 Draw up job descriptions for all staff concerned and for any outside consultants.

Stage 5 Draw up a training and development plan, including objectives, timescale and resources.

Stage 6 Monitor the effectiveness of actions carried out at the above five stages.

Activity

Tick those skills you need

— to understand more fully
— to train staff to acquire.

JOB AIDS 95

Below is a list of where you will find more information about these skills in the Guides. All the skills are described in practice in the case-studies in Volume 1, *Open Learning in Action*.

Heading	Skills	Relevant volume
Managing	team-building	3, 5, 7
	marketing	3, 5, 7
	decision-making	3, 5, 6, 7 (decisions have to be made throughout and in all activities
	liaising	Mainly 5, but also 3, 7
	planning	5 (general planning/organizing)
	organizing	3 (planning/organizing the support system)
		6 (planning/organizing the package)
		7 (planning/organizing the production process)
	prioritizing	3, 5, 7
	supervising	
	monitoring	5 (general)
		3 (support system)
		7 (production process)
	diagnosing where and when help is needed	5
	piloting	5 (whole system)
	validating	3 (support system)
	evaluating	2, 7 (package)
	modifying and updating the scheme	
Supporting learners	informing	3
	advising	
	guiding	
	tutoring	
	counselling	
Preparing and producing learning packages	analysing need	2, 5, 6
	writing objectives	2, 5, 6
	writing interactive features	2, 6
	adapting existing packages	8
	selecting media	8
	authoring	2, 6, 7, 8
	editing	6, 7
	designing	6, 7
	producing	6, 7
	delivering	5, 6, 7

96 WHAT IS OPEN LEARNING?

> *Key to Open Learning Guides mentioned*
> 2. *How to Help Learners Assess Their Progress: writing objectives, self-assessment questions and activities*
> 3. *How to Tutor and Support Learners*
> 5. *How to Develop and Manage an Open-Learning Scheme*
> 6. *How to Communicate with the Learner*
> 7. *How to Manage the Production Process*
> 8. *How to Find and Adapt Materials and Select Media*

Key activities

What activities will staff carry out in open learning, using these skills? Page 24 shows how these are grouped in the toolkit. This is a simplified version of a diagram reproduced in Volume 5, *How to Design and Manage an Open-Learning Scheme*. The detailed activities relating to each of the topics are then set out as shown on p 98.

The *Toolkit* gives further information on what each key activity might involve, as in the example below.

1.7 Clarify management structure	Responsibility for policy; responsibility for day-to-day running of scheme; role of any steering or advisory group; reporting arrangements; divisions of responsibility within scheme; liaison with any outside bodies, e.g. funders; responsibility for monitoring, updating, review; liaison with, control of, outside suppliers of services

The key activities are covered in the following volumes of this series (only major references are given).

Heading	Key activity	Relevant volume
Planning	Clarify target groups	2, 3, 5, 6
	Identify learning needs	2, 3, 5
	Establish the aims of the scheme	2, 5
	Get commitment to the scheme	3, 5
	Choose learning methods	3, 5, 6
	Choose assessment methods	2, 3, 5
	Clarify management structure	5, 7
	Draw up a schedule	5, 7
	Design administrative systems	3, 5, 7
Package	Decide your objectives	2, 5, 7, 8
	Find and select existing packages	8
	Adapt packages as necessary	2, 8
	Select media	6, 8
	Plan your own package	2, 5, 6, 8
	Author your package	2, 6, 8
	Edit and try out the package	6, 7
	Produce your package	6, 7

Support	Decide what support your learners will need	3
	Identify and brief those best suited to provide this support	3
	Decide how best to offer this support	3
	Provide feedback and assessment	2, 3, 6
	Help learners to learn	2, 3, 6
Management	Manage resources	3, 5, 7
	Choose and train staff	3, 5, 7
	Market	5
	Choose suitable delivery systems	3, 5, 6, 8
	Maintain records	3, 5, 7
	Monitor the scheme	5, 6, 7
	Review the scheme	5, 6, 7

Key to Open Learning Guides mentioned
2. *How to Help Learners Assess their Progress: writing objectives, self-assessment questions and activities*
3. *How to Tutor and Support Learners*
5. *How to Develop and Manage an Open-Learning Scheme*
6. *How to Communicate with the Learner*
7. *How to Manage the Production Process*
8. *How to Find and Adapt Materials and Select Media*

Plans of action

The toolkit goes on to show how these key activities can be planned and controlled by means of two types of plans of action. The column headings of the two types of plans are given here:

Action plan 1

Activity
Time-scale
Procedure
Person responsible
Budget
Notes

Action plan 2

Procedures in order of priority
Time-scale
Date achieved
Estimated cost
Actual cost
Notes

A **Activity**
Identify three activities currently of importance in your own learning scheme and then prepare first drafts of both action plan 1 and action plan 2. If you need further guidance refer to the completed examples in the *Toolkit*.

Key Activities Chart

1. Planning

1.1 Clarify target groups	1.2 Identify learning needs	1.3 Establish the aims of the scheme	1.4 Get commitment to the scheme	1.5 Choose learning methods	1.6 Choose assessment methods	1.7 Clarify management structure	1.8 Draw up a schedule	1.9 Design administrative systems

2. The Package

2.1 Decide your objectives	2.2 Find and select existing packages	2.3 Adapt packages as necessary	2.4 Select media	2.5 Plan your own package	2.6 Author your package	2.7 Edit and try out the package	2.8 Produce your package	2.9

3. Support

3.1 Decide what support your learners will need	3.2 Identify and brief those best suited to provide this support	3.3 Decide how to offer this support	3.4 Provide feedback and assessment	3.5 Help learners to learn	3.6	3.7	3.8	3.9

4. Scheme management

4.1 Manage Resources	4.2 Choose and train staff	4.3 Market	4.4 Choose suitable delivery systems	4.5 Maintain records	4.6 Monitor the scheme	4.7 Review the scheme	4.8	4.9

Section Eight. Booklist and Glossary to the Open Learning Guides

Booklist for the Open Learning Guides

Bååth, J, 'A list of ideas for the construction of distance education courses', pp 63–80, of Holmberg, B, and Bååth, J, *Distance Education: a short handbook*, Malmö: Liber-Hermods, 1982, reprinted in *Distance Education: international perspectives*, ed Sewart, D, Keegan, D, and Holmberg, B, Croom Helm, 1983. This is a useful collection of ideas for devices to build into materials to help learners master course objectives.

Bacon, G and Warren, J, *Computer-Assisted Management of a FlexiStudy Scheme*, Telford College of Further Education, published by the Scottish Council for Educational Technology in its Open Learning Papers series OLP 303, April 1984. See, too, *The Open Learning Unit at Kingsway Technical College* by John Mooney, OLP 103, March 1984. Both available from SCET, Dowanhill, 74 Victoria Crescent Road, Glasgow, G12 9JN.

Bagley, B and Challis, R, *Inside Open Learning*, Further Education Staff College, 1985. This is a fuller version of Birch, D and Latcham, J, *Flexible Learning in Action*.

Baker, Michael, 'The fast feedback system' in *Teaching at a Distance* No. 24, Open University, 1983.

Bates, A W, 'Broadcast television' in *The Role of Technology in Distance Education*, see below.

Bates, A W, 'Learning from audio-visual media', pp 33–58 of the Institutional Research Review, No. 1, *Student Learning from Different Media in the Open University*, Spring 1982.

Bates, A W, 'Resources for learning', *The Times Educational Supplement*, 20 April, 1984.

Bates, A W (ed), *The Role of Technology in Distance Education*, Croom Helm/St Martins Press, 1984.

Bates, A W, 'Trends in the use of audio-visual media in distance-education systems' in *Distance Education: international perspectives*, ed Sewart, D, Keegan, D, and Holmburg, B. Croom Helm, 1983.

Beck, J and Burton, J, *Prestel and Microviewdata in Education: a training course*, Council for Educational Technology, 1985. The eight modules can be combined to provide the basis of a two- or three-day workshop or they can be presented as a series of evening sessions.

Beveridge, W T, *Educational Computer Package Evaluation and Design*, Scottish Microelectronics Development Programme, Dowanhill, 74 Victoria Crescent Road, Glasgow, G12 9JN, June 1982. This is of particular relevance to readers using the computer as a medium. It is very short, full of good sense and the best thing we have read on how to design user-friendly educational software.

Birch, D W and Latcham, J, *Accounting for Academic Staff Resources for the Support of Open Learning*, Working Paper 1605, Further Education Staff College, Coombe Lodge, Blagdon, Bristol BS18 6RG.

Birch, D and Latcham, J, *Flexible Learning in Action*, Further Education Unit, 1984a. Contains useful analysis of aspects of flexibility and the implications of this for teachers and management structures in further education. Three case studies exemplify the principles. Obtainable from the DES Publications Despatch Centre, Honeypot Lane, Canons Park, Stanmore, Middlesex HA7 1AZ.

Birch, D W and Latcham, J, *Managing Open Learning*, Further Education Staff College (address above), 1984. This volume in the Further Education Staff College series 'Management in Colleges' will help further education colleges deal with the management issues faced when open learning is introduced. It includes chapters on using learning materials, tutoring, costing, managing innovation and has detailed appendices on (eg) costing and Burnham units.

Birch, D W and Latcham, J, *Some Aspects of Resource Management*, Working Paper 1611, Further Education Staff College (address above), 1982.

Bloom, B, *Handbook of Formative and Summative Evaluation of Student Learning*, McGraw-Hill, 1971.

Boydell, R H, *A Guide to Job Analysis*, British Association for Commercial and Industrial Education, 16 Park Crescent, London W1N 4AP, 1973.

Brew, Angela and Batten, Mary Anne, 'Levels of thinking and Open University study' in *Teaching at a Distance* No. 20 (pp 29–36), Open University, 1981. This is a thought-provoking account of an experiment which showed that Open University students can find it very difficult to distinguish levels of meaning in a text — for example, to recognize an 'example' from the 'theory' it is supposed to exemplify. It shows that writers of open-learning material in failing to perceive this are confusing rather than helping learners. The article can well be read alongside Northedge, listed below.

Briggs, J (ed), *Instructional Design: principles and applications*, Educational Technology Publications, New Jersey, 1977. A sound, comprehensive text — for the advanced reader!

British Gas, *Systems Approach to Training*. Available from the Training and Development Department, British Gas, 3 Grosvenor Crescent, London SW1X 7EE.

British Rate and Data (BRAD). Published monthly and obtainable from 76 Oxford Street, London W1N 9FD. This lists all British magazines, journals and newspapers, with their advertising rates.

Brookfield, S, 'Independent learning and correspondence students' in *Teaching at a Distance* No. 22, The Open University, 1982.

BTEC, *Open Learning Guidance Pack,* OL 83/1, March 1983. Available from the Business and Technician Education Council, 168–173 High Holborn, London, WC1. These guidelines have been put together to help those who wish to develop open-learning schemes for BTEC validation.

Burton, J and Taylor, J, *Educational Viewdata: start-up and user guides,* Council for Educational Technology, 1985. These materials comprise two guides and an accompanying disc of viewdata examples.

Calder, J, 'Adult learning and continuing education' in *Institutional Research Review,* No. 1, 1982. Available from the Open University, Walton Hall, Milton Keynes, MK7 6AA. This discusses the way in which other audiences than those originally intended take up and use open-learning materials.

Challis, R E, *Curriculum Evaluation in Further Education,* Working Paper 1339, Further Education Staff College (address above), June 1979. A useful source of ideas for readers in further education who wish to evaluate their schemes.

City and Guilds of London Institute, *The Manual of Objective Testing,* 1977.

Construction Industry Training Board, *Computer Assisted Training,* Management Training Series XA 618. A refreshingly simple, practical introduction to the topic.

Council for Educational Technology Information Sheet No. 7, 'Teleconferencing' (free), May 1985. (CET, 3 Devonshire St, London W1N 2BA.)

Council for Educational Technology Information Sheet No. 6, 'Copyright' (free), comprising:
(i) 'The use of copyright printed material for educational purposes'
(ii) 'Copyright and the copying of sound recordings for educational purposes'
(iii) 'Copyright and computers'
(iv) 'Off-air recording of broadcast programmes for educational purposes'
(v) 'Protection of computer programs'
(vi) 'Copyright and the copying of films'
This CET publication provides a useful guide and summary of the current legal position. (Address above.)

CET/FEU/FESC, *Information Technology and Educational Development.* Conference paper given at an invitation conference sponsored by the Council for Educational Technology, the Further Education Unit and the Further Education Staff College in March 1984.

Crabb G, *Copyright Agreements between Employers and Staff in Education*, Council for Educational Technology, 1979 (free from the above address).

Crabb, G, *Copyright Clearance: a practical guide* (Guidelines 2) Council for Educational Technology, 1981. This is the most readable and comprehensive guide to copyright clearance for educational purposes.

Daniel, J S, 'Independence and interaction in distance education: new technologies for home study' in *Programmed Learning and Educational Technology*, Volume 20, No. 3, August 1983. An up-to-date summary of how interaction might occur in open learning, with particular reference to new technological developments.

Davies, Ivor K, *Objectives in Curriculum Design*, McGraw-Hill, 1976.

Davies, T Charles, *Open Learning Systems for Mature Students* (Working Paper 14), Council for Educational Technology, 1977. The first CET publication on open learning, now out of print.

Day, H, *Self Instruction: an approach to staff training*, HMSO, 1984. This guide is produced by the Cabinet Office (Management and Personnel Office). It is a fascinating account of the many uses to which open learning is put in the Civil Service. The book has a full discussion of the advantages of open learning and it shows how cost-effective this form of training can be. Obtainable from HMSO bookshops.

Dean, C and Whitlock, Q, *A Handbook of Computer-Based Training*, Kogan Page' 1983. In a very short time this has established itself as the standard work on CBT.

Dean, C and Whitlock, Q, 'Computer-based training' in *The Personnel and Training Databook*, Kogan Page, 1985. Summarizes all the major considerations involved in this form of open learning, based on the authors' considerable experience.

Department of Education and Science, *Education Observed: a review of the first six months of published reports by HM Inspectors*, DES, 1984.

Department of Education and Science, *Education Observed 2: a review of published reports by HM Inspectors on primary schools and 11–16 and 12–16 comprehensive schools*, DES, 1984. Copies of these two DES publications are available from DES Publications Despatch Centre, Canons Park, Honeypot Lane, Stanmore, Middlesex, HA7 1AZ.

Department of Education and Science, *The PICKUP Handbook*, HMSO, 1984.

The Direct Mail Handbook, 4th edition, Gower Publishing Company, 1983.

Doulton, A and Bayard-White, C, *Interactive Video*, The National Interactive Video Centre, 1985. A simple, clear introduction to the subject.

Downs, S and Perry, P, *Developing Skilled Learners: learning to learn in YTS*, MSC Research and Development, No. 22, Manpower Services Commission, 1984. This paper stresses the importance of developing learning skills, whatever the context of the curriculum.

Drake, M, 'The curse of the course team', *Teaching at a Distance* 19, Open University, Winter 1979.

Duchastel, P, 'Unbounded text' in *Educational Technology* XXII, 8, August 1982. This article suggests setting text on sheets 23 x 33 in (map size). One chapter of a book (12–16 pages) could go on this. The article discusses the advantages this gives (eg, enables the learner to overview, gives design flexibility) and disadvantages (eg, how to keep the sheets together).

Duchastel, P, 'Towards the ideal study guide', *British Journal of Educational Technology*, 14, 3, October 1983. This covers (i) the function of a study guide (orientation, task direction, learning assistance, self-assessment); (ii) study guide components — purpose, significance and goals; text reference; outline of the subject matter; questions on the subject matter; key words and phrases; application problems, assignment test — a self-administered quiz. A very helpful article.

Duke, J, *Interactive video: implications for education and training* (Working Paper 22), Council for Educational Technology, 1983. The first major publication on interactive video, now inevitably somewhat dated.

Durbridge, N, 'Audio cassettes' in Bates, A W (ed), 1984 (see above).

Elliott, G, *Video Production in Education and Training*, Croom Helm, 1984. A useful introductory text.

Ellson, D G, 'Tutoring' in *The Psychology of Teaching Methods*, 75th yearbook of the National Society for the Study of Education, Part I, University of Chicago Press, 1976.

Ely Resource and Technology Centre, *Costing and Pricing Learning Materials*, Council for Educational Technology, 1983.

Evans, N, *Post Education Society*, Croom Helm, 1984. This discusses the future and sees a major role for open learning, particularly because of its potential for furthering autonomy.

Evans, N, *The Knowledge Revolution*, Grant McIntyre Ltd, 1981. This book, subtitled 'Making the link between learning and work', argues — on the basis of USA experience — that work and learning can be brought closer together with positive benefits for employees, employers and academic institutions.

Evans, T, 'Communicating with students by audio tape' in *Teaching at a Distance* No. 25, Open University, Autumn 1984. One of a number of useful articles on media selection appearing in this journal.

Ferguson, C, *Individualised Learning: the total approach of a Canadian college,* Coombe Lodge Report, 14, 12, 1982a. Obtainable from the Further Education Staff College (address above). Contains the account of Holland College, referred to and quoted from in this Guide.

Ferguson, C T, *New Learning Systems: some Canadian approaches,* Coombe Lodge Report, 15, 8, published by the Further Education Staff College (address above), 1982b.

Field, J, *Course Research Researched,* Open University Institutional Research Review No. 2. Obtainable from Regional Academic Services, The Open University, Walton Hall, Milton Keynes MK7 6AA.

Fielden, J and Pearson, P K, *Costing Educational Practice,* Council for Educational Technology (address above), 1978.

Freeman, Richard, 'MAIL from the NEC' in *Teaching at a Distance* No. 24, Open University, 1983.

Freshwater, M, 'Developments in the application of new technology to the development of open learning', paper delivered in May 1984 to a conference in Israel on 'The impact of informatics on vocational and continuing education'. Copies available from the author at the Manpower Services Commission, Moorfoot, Sheffield, S1 4PQ. Contains analysis of degrees of openness under heads of structure, administration, access/delivery, method, materials and assessment.

Freshwater, M R and Oates, N, *'Can-Do' Cards and Profiles: tools for self-assessment,* MSC Training Studies, 1982: for a fuller description of the Can-Do principle and how to operate it. Available from the Manpower Services Commission, Moorfoot, Sheffield S1 4PQ.

Towards a Personal Guidance Base, FEU, 1983.
Supporting YTS, FEU, 1983.
Curriculum Opportunities, FEU, 1983.
All these are available from the Further Education Curriculum Review and Development Unit, Elizabeth House, York Road, London SE1 7PH.

Further Education Unit, *Competency in Teaching: a review of competency and performance-based staff development,* FEU, 1982 (address above). An introduction to and survey of the topic. This would be useful further reading after Sections Five and Seven of this Guide.

Further Education Unit, *Curriculum-Led Institutional Development. A working paper,* RP116, Further Education Staff College and National Institute for Careers Education and Counselling. At the time of writing, no report exists. But by the time you read this further information will be available. Write to FEU for more details (address above).

Further Education Unit, *Flexible Learning Opportunities*, FEU, September, 1983 (address above). This source is mentioned several times in the text of this Guide, especially in Section Two. The document identifies a number of dimensions of flexibility along which students in further education would be moving if their autonomy were increased.

Further Education Unit, *Setting Up and Running Flexible Learning Workshops: a manual for guidance*, FEU, 1986.

Further Education Unit, *Teaching Skills: towards a strategy of staff development and support for vocational preparation*, FEU, 1982 (address above). Discusses staff development requirements for vocational preparation. Cf. Section Seven.

Further Education Unit, *Tutoring*, FEU, 1983 (address above). Another useful source for staff development from the FEU.

Further Education Unit/Manpower Services Commission, *Implementing Open Learning in Local Authority Institutions*, FEU/MSC, 1986.

Gagné, R M and Briggs, L J, *Principles of Instructional Design*, Holt, Rinehart and Winston, 1974.

Geisert, Paul and Futrell, Mynga, *Evaluating classroom computer courseware*, (pp 97–103). Details available from Paul Geisert, 1158 5th Street, NE, Washington, DC. Offers useful checklists.

Greenfield, D, 'Practical kits' in Bates, A W (ed), *The Role of Technology in Distance Education*, Croom Helm, 1984.

Grimwade, J R, 'Issues in teleconferencing' in *Open Campus*, 9, 1984. Occasional Papers published by the Distance Education Unit, Deakin University, Victoria 3217, Australia.

Gronlund, Norman E, *Management and Evaluation in Teaching*, Macmillan, 1971.

Hall, C, *Editing for Everyone*, National Extension College, 1983.

Harding, Pamela, *Flexible Learning in Small Fifth and Sixth Forms*, National Extension College, 1985. Write to NEC, 18 Brooklands Avenue, Cambridge CB2 2HN also for a copy of its Schools Catalogue, an annotated list of learning packages suitable for use in schools.

Harris, N D C, Bell, C D and Carter, J E H, *Signposts for Evaluating*, Council for Educational Technology, 1981. A package for schemes wishing to take evaluation seriously.

Harris, D, *Preparing Educational Materials*, Croom Helm, 1979. This has a chapter on 'Modes of Learning', which compares the various media.

Hartley, J, *Designing Instructional Text*, Kogan Page, 1978. A standard text on the subject.

Heidt, E U, *Instructional Media and the Individual Learner*, Kogan Page, 1978. A standard text on media.

Holden, E F J, 'Selection of instructional media systems' in *Programmed Learning and Educational Technology* 12.5, September 1975.

International Extension College, *Administration of Distance-Teaching Institutions: a manual*, IEC, 1983. This contains three elements: a text outlining the main issues and including questions and activities; a volume of case studies, mostly drawn from international schemes, and a course production game. The package can be used by an individual or a small group; in a workshop or as a correspondence course. It is strongly orientated towards distance schemes and an overseas audience. It is obtainable from the International Extension College, Office 2, Dales Brewery, Gwydir Street, Cambridge, CB1 2LJ.

Jenkins, Janet, *Materials for Learning*, Routledge and Kegan Paul, 1981. This has a useful section on illustration, especially for packages to be used in third-world countries.

Jones, Ann, 'Computer assisted learning in distance education' in Bates, A W (ed), 1984 (see above).

Kelly, P and Ryan, S, *Using Tutor Tapes to Support the Distance Learner*, International Council for Distance Education, Volume 3, September 1983. This describes an Open University project in which tutors prepared audiotapes. It includes comments on how the students reacted and gives practical advice. A shorter but more accessible version of this is Bell, M (and others), 'Tutor tapes for tutorial support' in *Teaching at a Distance* No. 23, Open University, 1983.

Kirkland, G, *Argyll and Bute FlexiStudy Scheme*, SCET Open Learning Paper No. 203 (address above), May 1983.

Knapper, C K, *Evaluating Instructional Technology*, Croom Helm, 1980. This compares various media.

Knasel, E G, Watts, A G, Kidd, J M, *The Benefit of Experience: individual guidance and support within the Youth Opportunities Programme*, MSC Research and Development Series, No. 5, 1982. Available from the Manpower Services Commission, Moorfoot, Sheffield S1 4PQ.

Latcham, J, *Helping Agencies*, Coombe Lodge Information Bank Paper 1876, 1984. Obtainable from the Further Education Staff College (address above). Contains a useful list of organizations which can assist in setting up and running open learning.

Latcham, J, *Learning Materials for Open Learning in Further Education*, Coombe Lodge Working Paper 1606, 1981. Available from the Further Education Staff College (address above).

Latcham, J and Spencer, D C, *Learner Flexibility Profiles*, Working Paper 1612, published by the Further Education Staff College (address above), 1983. This helps readers to analyse their open-learning scheme: how 'open' or 'flexible' is it?

Laurillard, D M, *The Problems and Possibilities of Interactive Video*, IET Paper No. 223. Reprinted in *New Technologies for Distance Education*, O'Shea, T et al (eds), Harvester Press (forthcoming). This article gives a fascinating analysis of the potential of interactive video. It outlines the ideal self-learning situation — the informal, relaxed way in which we find things out. Interactive video has the potential to simulate this non-formal learning situation; the learner can use his own idiosyncratic way of asking questions, locating information and deciding sequence. *But* educators and trainers will have to organize material to facilitate this. At the moment much interactive video design is based on the trainer-directed tradition of computer-based training.

Laurillard, D M, *Interactive Video and the Control of Learning*, IET Paper No. 231. Published in *Educational Technology*, 236, 1984 (Educational Technology Publications, 140 Sylvan Avenue, Englewood Cliffs, NJ 07632, USA).

Leech, G and Murphy, P, 'Mathematicians and intensive course writing', *Teaching at a Distance*, 8, Open University, 1977.

Lewis, R, *Counselling in Open Learning*, National Extension College, 1980. This is the report of an experiment run by the NEC in Leeds. Distance learners were provided with support from a local generalist counsellor. The book contains sections on the needs of distance learners and a detailed discussion of 'drop-out'. Case studies of tutoring in action are included and readers of these Guides may also be interested in the section on the role of telephone contact. Available from NEC (address above).

Lewis, R, *How to Tutor in an Open-Learning Scheme: self-study version*, Council for Educational Technology, 1981.

Lewis, R, *How to Tutor in an Open-Learning Scheme: group-study version*, Council for Educational Technology, 1981.

Lewis, R, *How to Tutor with NEC*, National Extension College 1981. This package includes a tape and booklet and is available from the National Extension College (address above).

Lewis, R, *How to Write Self-Study Materials* (Guidelines 10), Council for Educational Technology, 1981. This is a short, well-illustrated writer's guide.

Lewis, R, 'Tutoring in open learning' in *Aspects of Educational Technology XVII*, Kogan Page, 1984.

Lewis, R, 'Preparation of learning materials and roles of tutors' in *Open Learning*, proceedings of a symposium held in 1982 by the Scottish Business Education Council. Available from SCOTBEC, 22 Great King Street, Edinburgh.

Lewis, R and Paine, N with Lever, M, Robertson, F and Stevenson, A, *Team Working: a guide to management development groups* (for industrial users); *Studying Together* (for educational users); *Learning Together* (for study circles and informal learning groups). These three guides to self-help groups are published by the National Extension College (1985) (address above).

Lister, P, *The Coventry Computer-Based Learning Project*. Manpower Services Commission, December 1983. The report of the steering group of the Coventry Computer Based Learning Project using Plato. This contains many useful insights and is, at the time of writing, available free from MSC, Moorfoot, Sheffield, S1 4PQ.

Mager, Robert J, *Preparing Instructional Objectives*, Fearon, 1962.

Manwaring, G, *Sequences and Strategies*, Dundee College of Education, 1978. Available from Dundee College of Education, Gardyne Road, Broughty Ferry, Dundee, DD5 1NY. This discusses ways of sequencing the presentation of content within a course.

Manwaring, G, *What is 'Educational Technology'?*, Dundee College of Education (address above), 1983.

Marketing Solutions/Open Tech Unit, *A Guide to Marketing for Open Tech Projects*, Manpower Services Commission, 1985. The first book to be published dealing explicitly with how to market open learning. Available from MSC (address above).

McConnell, D, 'Cyclops shared-screen teleconferencing' in Bates, A W (ed), 1984 (see above).

Monk, J and O'Shea, T, 'Planning and role-differentiation in course production', *Teaching at a Distance* 19, Open University, Summer 1981.

Morris, A, *Writing Study Guides*, Council for Educational Technology, 1984.

Mullett, Tony, 'Feedback on T101' in *Teaching at a Distance* 24, Open University, 1983.

National Computing Centre, CBT Library Module 3, CBT Case Histories, NCC. This series of NCC modules is an important source for readers wishing to keep up to date with computer-based training.

National Extension College, *FlexiStudy: an introductory pack*. This includes a range of documents on FlexiStudy including the *FlexiStudy Manual*, *The Student's Guide* and *Your Questions Answered*. For details, write to NEC (address above).

National Extension College, *Supporting Open Learners*, sponsored by the Manpower Services Commission and produced by NEC in association with Glass Training Ltd, 1985.

National Extension College/Manpower Services Commission, *The Open Learning Toolkit: a development aid for managers*, NEC, 1985. This is a practical aid for anyone with management responsibility for an open-learning scheme. We refer extensively to it in Section Seven. The *Toolkit* is a companion to this series of Guides. Obtainable from NEC (address above).

National Economic Development Office/Manpower Services Commission, *Competence and Competition. Training and Education in the Federal Republic of Germany, the United States and Japan*. A report prepared by the Institute of Manpower Studies for the NEDO and the MSC and published by the NEDO, 1984.

Neville, C with Fearon, H and Wagner, L, *Development and Use of Materials for In-Service Training of Teachers* (Working Paper 21), Council for Educational Technology, 1982. See particularly Leslie Wagner's Coventry costing study in this volume.

Non-copyright graphics are supplied by the Graphics Communication Company, Maidstone, Kent.

Northedge, Andy, 'Some thoughts on the process of teaching and learning', internal Open University document, October 1979. Write to the author, Institute of Educational Technology, The Open University, Walton Hall, Milton Keynes MK7 6AA.

Open University, *Educational Guidance. A new service for adult learners*, OU, 1984. Available from The Open University, Fairfax House, Merrion Street, Leeds LS2 8JU. This is a manual for those wishing to set up and run an educational guidance service.

Open University, *How to Develop a Self-Instructional Package*, 1979. Available from The Open University, Walton Hall, Milton Keynes MK7 6AA.

Open University Centre for Continuing Education, *On the Line*, 1983. Available from the Learning Material Service, Centre for Continuing Education, The Open University, PO Box 188, Milton Keynes MK3 6HW.

Open Tech Unit of the Manpower Services Commission publishes *Open Tech News* (quarterly). Also available are: *The Open Tech Task Group Report* (June 1982) and *The Open Tech Programme Explained* (June 1984). The following papers have also been published: *The Open Tech: Why, What and How* by George Tolley; *Case Studies of Training Needs in the South East: Southtek report*; *Concepts and Strategies for Open Learning* by John Twining. All are available from the Manpower Services Commission (address above).

Paine, N, *How to Write Self-Assessment Questions*, Open Learning Paper No. 302. Scottish Council for Educational Technology (address as above), 1983. A short and very accessible guide to writing self-assessment questions.

Paine, N, 'Information technology' in *Educational Training and the New Technologies*, Tucker, J (ed), Kogan Page, 1984.

Paine, N, 'Information technology using open learning: interactivity analogue' in *Aspects of Educational Technology XVII*, Shaw, K E (ed), Kogan Page, 1984.

Paine, N, *Open Learning and Information Technology: the interactivity analogue*, Open Learning Paper No. 401, Scottish Council for Educational Technology (address above). In spite of the title, this is well worth reading. It points out that use of new technology is no guarantee of a good open-learning package. Designers and writers of computer software are not exempt from the principles of good educational technology.

Paine, N, 'Which button do I push?' (the use of video in open learning) in *Distance No Object*, HMSO, 1982.

Parsloe, E, *Interactive Video*, Sigma Technical Press, 1984. A useful compendium of information on all aspects of interactive video including the technical.

Percy, K *et al*, *Post-initial education in the North West of England* in Reader 2 of Open University Education for Adults Course, (ed) Tight, M, *Educational Opportunities for Adults*, Croom Helm/The Open University 1983. This includes an analysis of the failure of the education system to carry out adequate marketing.

Perraton, H, *The Cost of Distance Education*, International Extension College (address above), 1982.

Perraton, H, *Training Teachers at a Distance*, Commonwealth Secretariat, 1984. Available from Commonwealth Secretariat, Marlborough House, London, SW1Y 5HX.

Perraton, H and Jenkins, J, *The Invisible College*, International Extension College, 1980. This describes the setting up of the National Extension College. It contains interesting insights into the distance variant of open learning. Obtainable from IEC, Dales Brewery, Gwydir Street, Cambridge.

Perry, W, *Open University*, Open University Press, 1976. This describes the early days of the OU.

Riley, Judith, 'The problems of drafting distance-education manuscripts', 'The problems of revising drafts of distance-education manuscripts', and 'An explanation of drafting behaviours in the production of distance-education manuscripts'. Three articles in the *British Journal of Educational Technology*, 15, 3, 1984. These articles describe how authors set about the tasks of drafting and revising manuscripts, including the ways in which they use, or ignore, criticism of their work.

Robinson, B, 'Telephone teaching' in Bates, A W (ed), 1984 (see above).

Rogers, C, *Freedom to Learn in the Eighties*, Merrill, 1983. This book is included as a salutary reminder that the job of the tutor is to help the learner to develop autonomy. Rogers gives an excellent description of the tutor as facilitator and summarizes the key skills as genuineness, a positive valuing of other people and the ability to empathize with the learner.

Rogers, Wendy Stainton, 'The alternative use of Open University learning materials', internal Open University document. This describes transformation (take bits from original materials and alter them, eg, by using different media); selection (use only bits of the original); augmentation (generate new materials to cover local circumstances); integration (weld together the adapted package). A revised version of this paper appeared in *Teaching at a Distance* 24, Autumn 1983, as 'The uses of materials', but this unfortunately omitted many of the more interesting points from the original Open University paper.

Romiszowski, A J, *The Selection and Use of Instructional Media*, Kogan Page, 1974. The standard work on media selection. Useful if you are not daunted by the degree of elaboration used.

Rowntree, Derek, *Assessing Students. How shall we know them?* Harper and Row, 1977.

Rowntree, Derek, *Developing Courses for Students*, McGraw-Hill, 1981. An authoritative text on educational technology written in a very accessible style.

Rowntree, D, *Educational Technology in Curriculum Development*, Harper and Row, 1982.

Russell, J and Latcham, J, *Curriculum Development in Further Education*, Further Education Staff College (address above), 1979.

Russell, T J, *A Workshop on the Writing and Evaluation of Multiple-Choice Items*, Coombe Lodge Workbook No. 1330, 1979.

Russell, T J, *A Workshop on the Writing of Learning Objectives*, Coombe Lodge Working Paper 1331, Further Education Staff College (address above).

Schramm, W, *Big Media, Little Media*, Sage, Beverly Hills, 1977. A standard source.

Scottish Council for Educational Technology, *Open Learning Directory* (annual). Includes sections on what open learning is and how to choose a course. The Directory lists over 450 learning opportunities in Scotland. Obtainable from SCET (address above).

Scottish Education Department, *16–18s in Scotland. An Action Plan. Guide for parents and students*, 1984. Available from Scottish Education Department, 16–18 MDU, Room 4/25, New St Andrew's House, Edinburgh EH1 3SY.

Scottish Open Tech Training and Support Unit, Scottish Business Education Council Open Tech Project, Open Learning Small Business (Tourism), 'Training Course for Writers', Dundee College of Education (Crown Copyright), 1984. A very sound course provided with or without a tutor for schemes requiring a systematic 'distance' approach to writer training.

Scottish Open Tech Training and Support Unit, *Writing Materials for the Self-Instructional Unit*, 1984. A self-study text, with assignments. Contact T W Fyfe, Dundee College of Education, Gardyne Road, Broughty Ferry, Dundee, DD5 1NY, for details of availability.

Spencer, D C, *An Open-Learning Scheme at Harrogate College of Arts and Adult Studies*, Coombe Lodge Working Paper 1698, 1982. A description of the way the Harrogate OWTLET scheme works. Available from Further Education Staff College (address above).

Spencer, D C, *Thinking About Open Learning Systems* (Working Paper 19) Council for Educational Technology, 1980. A useful early analysis of open learning.

Stanford, J, 'A one-person course team', *Teaching at a Distance* 18, Open University, 1980.

Stratton, N J, 'Recurrent faults in objective test items' in *Teaching at a Distance* 20, Open University, 1981.

Stringer, M, 'Lifting the course team curse', *Teaching at a Distance* 18, Open University, Winter 1980.

Tavistock Institute, *Guide to Self-Evaluation of Projects*, Tavistock Institute of Human Relations, Belsize Lane, London, NW3 5BA, 1984. It is written specifically for Open Tech projects, but is useful generally.

Thompson, V, Brown, C, Knowles, C, *Videotex in Education: a new technology briefing*, Council for Educational Technology, 1982.

Tomlinson, K R, 'Media resource centres' in Bates, A W (ed), 1984 (see above). An analysis of ways in which libraries will need to adapt to act as support centres for open and distance students.

Tough, A, *The Adult's Learning Projects*, Ontario Institute for Studies in Education, 1979. Tough's work (this and following) decribes the learning projects adults regularly engage in, often without the support of any professional teacher or trainer.

Tough, A, *Intentional Changes*, Follett, 1982.

Tough, A, *Learning Without a Teacher*, Ontario Institute for Studies in Education, 1967.

Tough, A, *Why Adults Learn*, Ontario Institute for Studies in Education, 1968.

Training Officer (The), 'Audio visual aids in training', Marylebone Press, 1982. This selection of articles from *The Training Officer* gives much practical advice on how to make and use such media as audiocassettes, videocassettes and overhead projectors.

Twining, J, *Concepts and Strategies*, Open Tech Paper No. 3, Manpower Services Commission, 1984. Available from MSC (address above).

BOOKLIST FOR THE OPEN LEARNING GUIDES 115

Twining, J (ed), *Open Learning for Technicians,* Stanley Thornes, 1982. This is still the best available guide to open learning in technical subjects in colleges.

Waterhouse, P, *Managing the Learning Process,* McGraw-Hill, 1983. The Council for Educational Technology ran a project to promote open learning in schools, under the title 'Supported self-study'. The following books, the first a collection of case studies and the second a manual, are essential reading if you are working in schools.

Waterhouse, P, *Supported Self-Study in Secondary Education* (Working Paper 24), Council for Educational Technology, 1983.

Waterhouse, P, 'Preparing assignments in supported self-study', Supported Self-Study Occasional Paper 3, Council for Educational Technology, February 1984.

Waterhouse, P, *Supported Self-Study: a handbook for teachers,* Council for Educational Technology, 1983. The best available handbook for setting up open-learning arrangements in schools.

Watson, David, 'The Oxford Polytechnic Modular Course 1973–83: a case study' in *Journal for Higher Education,* 9, 1, 1985.

Wedermeyer, Charles, *Learning at the Back Door,* University of Wisconsin, 1981. An analysis of open learning; very useful for readers who want to take further the issues raised in this book — particularly the philosophical issues.

Wellington, J, 'Aid to intuition', *The Times Educational Supplement,* 18 May 1984. A useful checklist for selecting software.

Whitaker, P D, Roach, D K et al, *Video Systems* (User Guide 1), Council for Educational Technology, 1984.

Williams, Gareth and Woodhall, Maureen, *Independent Further Education,* Policy Studies Institute, XLV, 581, June 1979. A survey of private provision.

Winders, R, 'The Plymouth Audioconferencing Network' in *Teaching at a Distance* 25, Autumn 1984. This article describes the Plymouth Audioconferencing Network which at the time of writing — April 1985 — is beginning to produce some useful training material for teleconferencing. Contact Ray Winders, Director, PACNET, Learning Resources Centre, Plymouth Polytechnic, Drake Circus, Plymouth PL4 8AA.

Zorkoczy, P, 'Teletext systems' in Bates, A W (ed), 1984 (see above).

Glossary for the Open Learning Guides

This glossary includes the definitions of all terms used in the Open Learning Guides. It is thus comprehensive. Each of the volumes (except Volume 1, *Open Learning in Action*) has a glossary of the terms used in that particular volume.

Access devices. Means provided by writers to enable the learner to find those parts of the *Chunk* that he needs; access devices include lists of *Objectives*, summaries and *Self-Assessment Questions*.

Activity. An opportunity to apply learning to the world outside the package.

Advice. See *Support*.

Affective (used of the curriculum). The area of the curriculum involving feelings, attitudes and emotional responses.

Aim. A general statement of the intention of the planner or writer (See *Goal* and *Objective*).

Assessment. The measurement of learner performance; this may be formal or informal, exact or rough and ready, carried out by the learner himself (*Self-Assessment*) or by others. See *Formative and Summative Assessment; Self-Assessment Question*.

Assignment. A piece of work completed by a learner and handed or sent to a tutor for comment and assessment (also called *Tutor-Assessed Question*).

Author. The person who originates material for the learning package, eg, in the form of text, script or software program.

Authoring system/language. A specialized programming language for creating computer-based packages. An authoring language enables educators, trainers and others to construct computer-based training programs. Some authoring languages can be used by people without programming experience or knowledge of computing. An authoring language sits within a *System* which provides facilities such as checking and file-handling.

Binding. The method of holding together the pages in a book. The most common methods are 'perfect binding': by this method the pages are simply stuck to the spine of the book's cover (as with a paperback book); 'sewn binding': this is similar to perfect, but the quality is somewhat stronger because the pages are also sewn together before they are stuck to the spine of the book's cover; 'saddle-stitched binding': this is used for relatively small books: the pages are stapled twice along the book's spine; 'comb binding': the pages of the book are held together by means of a plastic or metal spiral; this has the advantages that the pages open flat and it is therefore particularly useful for manuals.

Branching. A term used to describe the process whereby the learner selects one particular option at a point in a learning programme.

Camera-ready artwork. This describes the pages that are passed to the printer for printing. In other words, all the typesetting, illustrations, page numbers, etc, have been put in place by the designer or paste-up artist, and have been checked by the proofreader.

Case-study. Presentation of real or imagined experience often, in an open-learning package, followed by self-assessment questions.

Checklist. A list of questions against which a learner can check progress towards carrying out a particular activity.

Chunk. Part of a package that forms a coherent learning experience: could be short (eg, *Segment*), longer (eg, *Module*) or at the level of the *Package* as a whole.

Cloze test. A method for checking the readability of a piece of text.

Coding. Entails the conversion of *Programmable ready material* (ie, the course on paper) into computer-based training format. A computer program is generated which makes it possible to present the course through the computer terminal.

Concept map. A visual representation of the ways in which the concepts in a package relate to each other.

Consultant. A person attached to a project, usually for a short time. A consultant can carry out a wide range of activities, eg, offer expert advice, carry out training, solve a problem.

Contact. Person-to-person communication by whatever means, eg, letter, telephone, face-to-face.

Core resource. Text (or equivalent in other media) around which an open-learning package is built.

Counselling. See *Support.*

Course. A planned learning experience. It may be tightly structured (eg, the Open University undergraduate programme) or loose (eg, a study circle); it may be long or short in duration; it may or may not lead to a qualification; it may be offered by an educational, industrial or other provider; it may be formal or informal. In industry the word *Programme* is sometimes used instead of *Course*. In these Guides *Scheme* and *Project* are used synonymously with *Course*.

Courseware. Learning material developed for use on a computer or computer-controlled system such as interactive video.

Copyediting. Checking the completed manuscript against the *House style,* eg, spelling, punctuation, captions. Preparing the manuscript for typing or typesetting.

Cyclops. Equipment, used mainly within the Open University, which allows a tutor to communicate with remote students via the telephone line. Visual information is displayed on a screen. The learner can annotate this by using a lightpen. In early systems Cyclops required two telephone lines for visual and audio communication. A more recent modification allows both these forms of communication to be transmitted on one telephone line.

Debugging. Checking a computer-based training module for any errors or inadequacies in design/coding.

Delivery. The ways in which a scheme provides the learner with materials and support.

Design. See *Development.*

Designer. A person who advises on, and/or carries out, the visual specification for a package — eg, illustrations, size of type, layout, cover.

Development. The process of planning a scheme; used synonymously with *Design* and *Planning.*

Developmental testing. The small-scale try-out of learning materials in draft, on members of the target population. A form of *Pilot.* Cf. also *Validation.*

Diagnostic test. Series of questions to enable the learner to decide which part of a *Package* he needs.

Distance learning. One kind of open learning. Distance learning implies the geographical separation of learner from tutor, as in correspondence courses. The learner is usually in touch with the tutor only by post or telephone though in some schemes residential periods of study are also offered.

Drop-out. A term used to describe the process by which a learner ceases to study within an open-learning scheme. The learner may consciously drop out or just drift into the position of non-contact with the provider.

Editor. An imprecise term for someone with particular responsibility for the package. The editor may have a relatively narrow role (eg, copyediting) or a very broad one (eg, to issue contracts and train authors). The editor may be responsible for seeing the *House style* is observed, checking technical accuracy and ensuring that the package is designed on sound learning principles. He or she may also supervise the production process, eg, devising and monitoring budgets and schedules.

Enrichment loops/sections. Extra parts of a *Chunk* providing further material for the able or advanced learner or for the learner who wishes to study a particular topic further. (See *Remedial loops/sections.*).

Enrolment. The process by which the learner joins a scheme.

Evaluation. The process of gathering information from various sources in order to investigate a scheme's performance and effectiveness. Often used interchangeably with 'monitoring', but evaluation generally implies a greater degree of detachment and is usually periodic.

Feedback. The provision of comment on a learner's performance either within the package or by some other means (eg, computer, tutor). In the package this may be called 'answer', 'response' or some similar name.

Field trial. Term used loosely to mean one or other form of *Pilot.* Sometimes used to describe the testing of materials on a very small group of learners (cf. *Developmental testing*); sometimes used to describe a more formal *Pilot* with larger numbers (cf. *Validation*).

Firmware. Either the software or courseware held on ROM chip. This allows more rapid access of the software by the computer. It therefore has a status between software (computer programs) and hardware (machinery in which the program is run).

FlexiStudy. An open-learning scheme run by the National Extension College in association with education and training institutions, usually colleges of further education. NEC is the main provider of learning materials and the institution is responsible for support.

Flowchart. A diagram showing a computer or video program. A flowchart is usually a series of different shaped boxes, some joined by lines.

Format. The open-learning features used in a package and the way these are shown.

Formative assessment. Assessment carried out during a scheme to help learners to manage their own learning; formative assessment provides feedback to learners on their performance.

Frame. This is used in two senses. The term originated in the days of teaching machines and referred to the text and/or picture the learner could see presented in the window or frame of the machine. Hence the most common use of *Frame* is as a synonym for 'screen' — the material presented on a single screen of a VDU. The other use of *Frame* is to describe a unit of instruction, ie, the teaching of a specific item within the lesson including the explanation, worked examples, learner activity and feedback. All this may often be possible to present on a single screen. But where it includes offline activity such as completing a task in a workbook or operating some apparatus, the *Frame* represents a learning step rather than a physical presentation device.

Gateway. A link which allows a viewdata system to access information from an external computer. Such links are transparent to the user. See also *Viewdata, Videotex* and *Teletext.*

Goal. A more specific statement than an *Aim.* A goal is expressed in terms of learning outcomes but not as specifically as an *Objective.*

Guidance. See *Support.*

HELP section. Part of a *Package* designed to help learners who have got into difficulty.

Highband. See *U-matic.*

House style. Instruction given to writers/editors by a publishing organization; the instructions cover such points as which spellings to use, how to record sources, (sometimes also called 'house rules').

Illustrator. The person who produces cartoons, sketches, technical pictures and who takes photographs for use in a *Package.*

Induction. The process by which a learner is helped to understand the requirements and mode of operation of a particular open-learning scheme.

Input. Information fed into the computer.

Interactive video. Term used to describe the linking of video and computer technologies. At a simple level it involves segmenting videotapes to play selected parts to the learner. At the most sophisticated level it involves full computer control of a disc allowing the student to access data, pictures (still or moving) as well as software.

Layout. The way in which words and illustrations are set out on the page or its equivalent (eg, computer screen).

Learner. Anyone learning in an open-learning scheme. In this series *Learner* is chosen as the generic term; cf. 'student', 'trainee', 'employee', 'customer', 'client', 'punter'. All these would be covered by the term *Learner*.

Learning materials. See *Package*.

Linear presentation. Presentation of learning material in a sequence which follows on frame by frame or page by page. It implies that there is no branching or learner choice in the way the material is presented.

Lowband. See *U-matic*.

MAIL. An abbreviation of Micro-Aided Learning, a computerized system developed by the National Extension College in 1983 to provide feedback for open learners.

Maintenance. Servicing a scheme. In Volumes 5 and 7 we discuss the maintenance of the package. Volume 3, *How to Tutor and Support Learners* describes the maintenance of the support system.

Management. The actions and processes necessary to ensure that learner needs are met and their objectives attained (cf. *Delivery*).

Manuscript. This describes the words provided (usually in typewritten form) by an author. Ideally a manuscript should be typed, double-spaced and single-sided, to leave space for editing.

MARIS. The Materials and Resources Information Service: an Open Tech project managed by the National Extension College for England and Wales and by the Scottish Council for Educational Technology for Scotland.

Marketing. The process of identifying, anticipating and satisfying customer requirements. When used in open learning the word implies a wide range of activities, of which promotion is only one.

Matching list. A question which presents two lists for the learner who has to match items in one list with those in the other.

Materials. See *Open-learning package*.

Medium/media. The means chosen for transmission of the package (eg, audiotape, print).

Menu. List of content and function of a computer program, enabling the user to select what he needs.

Microviewdata (sometimes called local viewdata). Software allowing users to create viewdata pages and databases themselves, using a microcomputer. The more sophisticated software packages enable other people to gain access to such databases, via the telephone line. See also *Viewdata*, *Videotex* and *Teletext*.

Module. A self-contained *Chunk* of learning, parts of a *Package*. Modules are often between 4 and 12 hours long. They may themselves be divided into smaller elements

GLOSSARY FOR THE OPEN LEARNING GUIDES 121

(Segments). Modular learning materials enable learners to choose which objectives they wish to cover and the sequences in which they wish to cover them. (Note that there is considerable variation between the terms used in different schemes to describe the elements into which a course is divided. For example, instead of *Package*, *Course* may be used; instead of *Module*, 'block' or 'unit'; instead of *Segment*, 'chapter' or 'section'.)

Monitoring. The regular scrutiny of the performance of the scheme, or part of a scheme, as it is running; checking the effectiveness of management procedures, learner support and learning materials. Often used interchangeably with *Evaluation*.

Multiple-choice question. A question which takes the form of a stem followed by a series of possible answers (options). Usually only one of these is correct (the key) and others are incorrect (the distractors).

Objective. A description of the purpose of a scheme expressed in terms of the capacities that the learner will acquire and demonstrate; a statement of learning outcomes. See *Aim* and *Goal*.

Offline edit. An initial edit usually carried out on lower format equipment; used as a check before the final edit on highband or one-inch equipment.

Offset litho. This is the modern method of printing. In effect, a photograph of the page is used to reproduce further copies. This may be very straightforward, using paper plates, or the process may be more complex, in which case a series of negatives is first prepared and these are then turned into metal plates.

Open-learning course/programme/scheme/system. 'Open-learning' is a term used to describe courses flexibly designed to meet individual requirements. It is often applied to provision which tries to remove barriers that prevent attendance at more traditional courses but it also suggests a learner-centred philosophy. Open-learning courses may be offered in a learning centre of some kind or most of the activity may be carried out away from such a centre (eg, at home).

Open-learning package/package/materials/materials. Specially prepared or adapted materials to enable the learner to study for a significant part of his time on his own.

OTTSU (Open Tech Training and Support Unit). An Open Tech project managed until April 1986 by the Council for Educational Technology.

Overview. The section at the beginning of a learning sequence which allows the learner to gain a quick insight into what lies before him.

Paste-up. This is the process of putting together camera-ready artwork — sticking the typesetting, pages, numbers, pictures, etc, on the right part of the page.

Photosetting. This is now the usual form of typesetting. Whereas a typesetting machine works very much like a normal typewriter, typing lines directly on a page with the help of a ribbon, the photosetter stores the words in the computer memory. These are then printed out either on film or paper. Either way, you finish up with a slightly better finished product.

Pilot. The trial of a *Scheme* or part of it before full operation, with the intention of collecting feedback, to assess its performance and decide on any modification necessary; 'trial', 'test' and 'try-out' are used synonymously with *Pilot.* See also *Validation, Field trial* and *Developmental testing.*

Planning. See *Development.*

Plates. These enable us to print multiple copies. Paper plates are simply direct replicas of the camera-ready artwork. Metal plates are made from the negative of the camera-ready artwork. Paper plates are much cheaper but are generally used only once, whereas metal plates can be used again and again. In either case, parts of the surface of the plate reject ink, so that when the plate is pressed against paper only the words and pictures will be printed.

Post-test. Set of questions that enable the learner to check how successfully he has mastered the objectives of a particular *Chunk.*

Practical kit. Any hardware issued for use at home for learning purposes. A kit contains essential components not likely to be found in the home; thus a microscope would be included in a kit but not a pair of scissors.

Pre-entry counselling. The advice and support a learner receives before joining an open-learning scheme.

Prerequisites. The knowledge, skills, etc, the learner needs before tackling a particular *Chunk.*

Pre-test. A series of questions that enable the learner to decide whether or not he needs to study a particular *Chunk* or part of it.

Program. A series of instructions (usually written in a programming language) which can be understood and obeyed by a computer.

Programmable ready material. A phrase first developed by users of the PLATO language. It refers to the pre-coding design documentation which the course designer develops. It will comprise the text and graphics to be presented to the learners and include a flowchart indicating the learner routeings appropriate to responses to both pre- and post-tests and to feedback questions in the body of the lesson. Almost always the text will be written on screen design sheets. These sheets are printed with a grid pattern of columns and rows to represent the screen presentation mode of the computer system in use. An author using Microtext on the BBC, for example, will usually write his text on squared screen design sheets of 40 columns by 23 rows.

Programme/learning programme. See *Course.*

Project. See *Course.*

Proofreading. Checking of typeset material to ensure instructions in the manuscript have been carried out. The later checking of corrections.

Provider/providing body. The institution, organization or individual responsible for making available a particular open-learning scheme (eg, British Telecom, the Open University, Sight and Sound — see Volume 1, *Open Learning in Action.*)

Psychomotor (used of the curriculum). The area of the curriculum involving physical skills/manipulation.

Remedial loops/sections. Extra parts of a *Chunk* provided for learners who experience difficulty.

Response analysis. The process of analysing a learner's reply to a question, carried out by the computer.

Review questions. Questions asked at the end of a *Chunk* to enable the learner to double-check his progress towards meeting *Objectives*.

Routeing. Guides the learner to appropriate parts of a package and the sequence in which these will be studied.

Scheme. See *Course*.

SCOTTSU. The Scottish Open Tech Training and Support Unit — an Open Tech project managed by Dundee College of Education.

Script. A production document containing the spoken soundtrack of a programme and linking this to the visual content.

Segment. Subdivision of a module.

Self-assessment question. Opportunity within the text that enables the learner to prepare for a learning experience; tests his understanding of a particular point; enters into dialogue with the package writer.

Self-check. One type of *Self-assessment question* enabling the learner to check his acquisition of a particular point or concept.

Self-help group. A group of learners who come together voluntarily to plan and implement a learning programme. Their objectives may be pre-set (eg, the syllabus of an examining body) or formulated by the learners themselves.

Signposting. Indications of where the learner has got to, come from and is going to: signposting helps the learner to orient himself.

Software. A *Program* or set of *Programs*.

Specification. A vital part of any production process: it provides all the details about the job, including length, number of words, number of pictures, type of printing, type of cover, type of binding, etc (or the equivalent details in a medium other than print). The specification helps all the people in the production process to plan and budget appropriately.

Split screen. A technique whereby the visual display unit or television screen is divided in two, four, or more sections electronically so that different kinds of information can be displayed in each section. Typically text is displayed in one part while a still or moving picture is displayed in another.

Storyboard. A series of illustrations providing a sequence of shots, showing the visual content of a programme.

Study guide. Material accompanying a core resource (eg, a textbook providing open-learning features such as *Objectives, Activities and Self-assessment questions*).

Summative assessment. Assessment carried out at the end of a scheme; the primary intention is to provide a record of performance rather than to help learners to manage their own learning.

Support. The arrangements made within an open-learning scheme to provide extra help to the learners to that already contained in the learning package. Support includes contact, advice, guidance, counselling, tutoring and the provision of practical experience.

System. See *Course.*

Target audience. The learners for whom a particular course has been prepared. They may be in education (students), training (trainees), work (employees) or others. See *Learner.*

Teleconference. A system whereby any number of telephone lines (up to 15) are linked together in order that a conference call can take place. Each of the participants can hear and speak with all of the other participants. There is usually a voice-switching mechanism in the linking bridge which allows only one participant to speak at a time.

Telesoftware. A means of storing and distributing materials — software, text and graphics — so that they can be received (downloaded) into the memory of the user's microcomputer through a viewdata or teletext system or over the radio (audio software). These materials can subsequently be stored on disc or cassette.

Teletext. A page-orientated information system using a particular style of frame presentation and transmitted in a fixed cyclical sequence via broadcast signals. These pages are identified by numbers and displayed, as selected, on a special television or a microcomputer with an adaptor. It is not possible for the user to send information back to such a system. CEEFAX and ORACLE are examples of teletext systems. See also *Videotex* and *Viewdata.*

Teletext simulator. This is a piece of *Software* which allows a small microcomputer to generate a database of teletext-type pages of information and save these pages on disc.

Teletutoring. Use of the telephone for *Tutoring* as opposed to general support or for the holding of general meetings.

Transformer. Person who turns conventional material into open-learning form.

Tutor. General term for the person in an open-learning system who is directly responsible for the learner. The tutor is usually a professional — an educator or trainer. His main task is to help the learner to acquire skills and strategies needed to become autonomous, usually through mastery of a particular subject area or skill. He is variously described as 'counsellor', 'mentor', 'coach', 'guide', 'trainer', 'supervisor' and 'godfather'.

Tutor-assessed question. A question answered by a learner and handed or sent to a tutor for comment and assessment.

Tutor notes. Instructions, guidance, etc, provided by a course writer to help tutors carry out their role in an open-learning scheme.

Typesetting. This is basically very similar to typewriting. Most typesetting machines can do tasks such as justifying the lines so that blocks of text have straight edges, and most also have a memory which enables their users to correct as they go.

U-matic. ¾in videocassette system, originally developed by Sony. This can be subdivided into (a) *Lowband* — the standard U-matic system, widely used in commercial and industrial applications, and (b) *Highband* — a U-matic system with an extended bandwidth, giving higher quality to broadcast standard.

Validation. The testing of an *Open-learning package* and/or other components of a *Scheme* in a real context, with a representative sample of the *Target audience*. In practice the words *Validation* and *Pilot* are often used interchangeably. See *Pilot* and *Developmental testing.*

Videocassette recorder (VCR). A videotape recorder which handles cassettes.

Visual display unit (VDU). An output device, similar in appearance to a television set.

Video Home System (VHS). A ½in videocassette system developed by the Japan Victor Company (JVC).

Videotex. The generic term to cover both *Teletext* and *Viewdata.*

Viewdata. An interactive page-orientated computer information storage and retrieval system using a particular style of frame presentation. These pages are stored in a tree structure to form a database. The provision of pages allows information to be easily located. PRESTEL is an example of a *Viewdata* system. See also *Videotex* and *Teletext.*

Workshop/Open-learning workshop. An *Open-learning scheme* based in a centre. The learner works in the centre, which holds materials. These can be used by the learner either by dropping in or by booking. (The word *Workshop* is also often used to describe short, participative training events.)

Youth Training Scheme (*YTS*). An initiative of the Manpower Services Commission, set up in 1983 to provide training, work experience and education for young adults.

Section Nine. Appendices

Appendices

CONTENTS
Appendix One. Other initiatives and resources
Appendix Two. Definitions

APPENDIX ONE· OTHER INITIATIVES AND RESOURCES
The Open Learning Guides complement other resources.

'Open Learning Toolkit'
The *Open Learning Toolkit* has already been mentioned several times. This is part of an MSC series on 'Trainer competencies for the 1990s'; other publications in this series will deal with the competencies needed to design and produce computer-based training (CBT) programmes.

Council for Educational Technology
CET has produced several publications to help organizations set up open learning. These include:

How to Write Self-Study Materials, Roger Lewis, 1981
How to Tutor in an Open-Learning Scheme (group and self-study versions), Roger Lewis, 1981
Signposts for Evaluating: a resource pack, N D C Harris, C D Bell and J E H Carter, 1981
'Making Open Learning Work', 1986. A series of short guides for learners, tutors and those who are responsible for, or administer, open-learning projects. CET's main office is at 3 Devonshire Street, London W1N 2BA (tel 01–636 4186). The Open Learning Unit is at Rooms 24–27, Prudential Buildings, Above Bar Street, Southampton SO1 0FG.

Further Education Unit
Another source of open-learning publications is the FEU; see, for example, the volumes on *Teaching Skills, Tutoring* and *Flexible Learning Opportunities* mentioned in the Booklist. FEU publications are available from the DES Publications Despatch Centre, Honeypot Lane, Canons Park, Stanmore, Middlesex HA7 1AZ.

MARIS
MARIS — the Materials and Resources Information Service — can provide you with help locating the resources you may need to develop open learning. MARIS also provides details of packages for use in open learning. You can contact MARIS at Bank House, 1 St Mary's Street, Ely, Cambs CB7 4ER (tel 0353 61284) if in England or Wales; or at SCET, Dowanhill, 74 Victoria Crescent Road, Glasgow, G12 9JN (tel 041–334 9314) if you work in Scotland.

Other sources

Other useful sources of publications and advice and information on open learning are:

— the Further Education Staff College, Coombe Lodge, Blagdon, Bristol BS18 6RG
— the National Extension College, 18 Brooklands Avenue, Cambridge CB2 2HN
— OTTSU (the Open Tech Training Support Unit), Rooms 24–27, Prudential Buildings, Above Bar Street, Southampton SO1 0FG
— the Open Tech Unit of the Manpower Services Commission, Moorfoot, Sheffield S1 4PQ
— the Scottish Council for Educational Technology, Dowanhill, 74 Victoria Crescent Road, Glasgow G12 9JN
— SCOTTSU (the Scottish Open Tech Training Support Unit), Dundee College of Education, Gardyne Road, Dundee, DD5 1NY.

Ask the above organizations for lists of their publications.

APPENDIX TWO· DEFINITIONS

Section One of this book defined 'open learning' as used throughout the Open Learning Guides. Many other items are used to mean much the same thing in practice. 'Open Learning' is rapidly becoming an umbrella term. Some of the terms used below place emphasis on different aspects of openness.

Directed private study: structured private study — the learner moves through a structured programme, paced by assignments, often using textbooks and study guides.

Distance learning: this usually implies considerable geographical distance between learner and the providing institution. The learner makes contact by post and telephone with the institution and with any tutor.

Drop-in learning (or 'open access'; 'workshop learning'; 'learning by appointment'): the learner visits (drops in, or books into) a centre, learns from the materials provided there and, usually, has access to counselling and other forms of support, such as diagnostic assessment.

Flexible learning: FEU synonym for 'open learning'.

FlexiStudy: learners are home-based, using specially prepared open-learning texts. Their tutor is based in a local college, teaching them at a distance using the post and telephone. But FlexiStudy students also come into their local college from time to time for tutorials and to use college facilities.

Independent learning: this term usually implies that the learner chooses not only pace and place but also purpose, learning style and strategy. There is thus a greater implied freedom and responsibility given to the learner than in *individualized learning:* the learner is *answerable* for more. The Council for National Academic Awards defines independent learning as 'learning through the student constructing and carrying out himself a programme of study to meet his own objectives' (CNAA, *Guidance on the validation of courses which makes significant use of resource-based learning'*). Cf. 'autonomous learning'; 'self-directed learning'; 'learner-directed training'; these seem synonymous with 'independent learning'.

Individualized learning: the learner works on materials tailored to his individual needs, capabilities and interests. In practice, the freedom given to the learner is restricted when compared with that given in *independent learning*. The learner may be able to choose pace and place of learning, and sequence, but not the objectives.

Resource-based learning: the learner has direct access to sources, eg, of information or stimulus, rather than their being mediated through a teacher. The phrase usually suggests learning from a range of media, not only from print.

Self-access learning: implies the learner takes the initiative and selects from a range of resources.

Self-study: general term for any scheme in which the learner is largely or totally dependent on specially prepared resources, with a minimum of tutorial support.

Student-negotiated learning: implies the presence of a tutor/trainer with whom the student negotiates; the phase implies a commitment to student-centredness; the negotiation may be over objectives, methods of realizing objectives, choice of content, assessment, or any other aspects of the learning process.

Supported self-study: 'an arrangement whereby a pupil pursues a whole course of study, or part of a course, through the use of structured learning materials, with tutorial support from a teacher. It can be regarded as an alternative to class teaching, or as a supplement to it. It can be organized on any scale: large enough to represent a transformation in the working philosophy of the school; or small enough to provide an enriching experience, with minimum upheaval' (Waterhouse, 1984). The learner is supported — by a tutor and a caring structure. See Waterhouse, Working Paper 24, pp 16–17 for a full discussion of the terms, as applied by the Council for Educational Technology to work in schools; eg, 'a helping activity concerned with personal growth and knowledge'.